Endorsements

If you want to be a better leader at work and home, you need to build discipline, not by doing more things, but by doing the right things. This book will show you how.

—Jon Gordon
17x Bestselling Author of *Training Camp: What the Best Do Better Than Everyone Else* and *The One Truth: Elevate Your Mind, Unlock Your Power, Heal Your Soul*

Craig's systems have given me the tools to stay focused at work so we scale faster while also giving me more quality time with my family.

—Sharran Srivatsaa
President, Real Brokerage Inc.

Craig Ballantyne is one of the most disciplined people I know. If you want to change your life, achieve more, and reach your peak potential, you need to work with Craig.

—Bedros Keuilian
Author of *Man-Up*

Goals without discipline are wishes; discipline without clarity is aimless. The most successful business leaders have a clear vision and the disciplines (routines) to make it a reality. Craig and Daniel's book will show you how.

—Verne Harnish
Founder, Entrepreneurs' Organization (EO), and Author of *Scaling Up*

Craig and Daniel's coaching has given me the tools to laser-focus my efforts at work so I have more time for my family every day. Their discipline systems have given me more time to do the things I love, as well as financial freedom.

—Isabel Price
Entrepreneur and homeschooling mom of 2

Creating standards for your life and making those standards nonnegotiable will be the key differentiator in living a successful, happy life or not. Craig has been a massive influence in my life, helping me with increasing the standards and expectations I hold for myself. His book will change your life for the better.

—Justin Colby
Founder of *The Entrepreneur DNA* Podcast

I work in a cut-throat industry. Being disciplined and maintaining high standards are key. Craig's systems have given me the edge to stay consistent and have big breakthroughs.

—Matt Del Negro
TV actor, *Sopranos, Mayor of Kingstown*

Craig and Daniel's systems and standards have not only helped me supercharge my productivity but also allowed me to pursue my biggest goals without sacrificing what matters most—my family and well-being. This book is a powerful roadmap to achieving true freedom, both professionally and personally.

—Shannon Logan
Entrepreneur and mom

Being an entrepreneur isn't for everyone. Tough days are inevitable—and periods of high anxiety and overwhelm constantly threaten our inner peace… and sanity. If you don't have the systems, discipline, and high standards for your personal AND company performance, you won't last long. Craig's books show you how to get through hard times and create a foundation for lasting success.

—Steven McBee
Entrepreneur and founder of McBee Meats
and star of *Dynasty: Real American Cowboys*

Discipline and standards—the formula for greatness. All the business success and revenue growth Daniel and Craig have helped me with is nice. Even better than that is how my wife, two sons, and team see me act in times of stress, adversity, and life challenges that matter to me most. Thanks for helping me grow as an individual and leader to continually show up as my best self.

—Dr. John Tait, MD
Founder of Origen Orthopedics, Tucson, AZ

Ten years ago, I started my online journey with the help of Craig. His systems and structure have helped me to scale my business to over eight figures, and still growing! Don't just read this book—take action on it, as it can change your life.

—Robby Blanchard
Founder of Commission Hero

The music industry is not for the faint of heart. Working with Craig was an important part of my journey that taught me the importance of discipline, strong leadership, and family life balance. 10/10 would recommend.

—Seth Mosley
Grammy-winning producer/writer, Nashville, TN

I've been following Craig for a decade and have worked with him directly for 5 years. Craig's methods helped me to write a book in 2 weeks, spend more time with my two boys, and quadruple my income in less than 2 years. This book can help you achieve more than you ever thought possible, all by actually doing LESS! Take these lessons and then apply them with ACTION, and you can experience life-changing results as well.

—Chris Larsen
Real Estate Investor and Author of *Next-Level Income*

Thanks to Craig's discipline systems, I went from being a personal trainer trapped in a J-O-B to setting up a new business that gave me the life of freedom I always wanted.

—Kate Vidulich
Chief marketing officer

I used Craig's discipline systems and morning routine to tackle my most important work. The results have far exceeded my expectations. I ended up writing the first draft of my first book in thirty-six days. This wouldn't have happened without the radical shifts that helped me reprioritize my most valuable energy to my most important activities. Simple yet insanely powerful. I wish I had done it sooner.

—Mike Zeller
Bestselling Author of *God + You Journal* and *The Genius Within*

Working with professional athletes is challenging. I need discipline and high standards every day. Craig Ballantyne is a fantastic resource for anyone who needs help developing the systems, processes, and discipline required to help you achieve the highest levels of performance in sport, in business, or in life.

—Matt Nichol
Strength Coach, Paragenix Systems, Toronto, ONT

Craig's game-changing systems and Daniel's relentless standards transformed the way I work—helping me harness my ADHD into laser-focused productivity and build unshakable discipline. If you're ready to stop spinning your wheels and start dominating what truly matters, this is your roadmap.

—Galel Fajardo
Coach for ADHD entrepreneurs

I am a female entrepreneur in a male-dominated industry, battling imposter syndrome, lack of experience, and self-doubt. Craig and Daniel's lessons on standards and discipline have had a huge impact—helping me navigate the most difficult challenges in growing my business.

—Kristy Black
CEO, Black Hydrovac

If you want to be successful in business and at home, you need level 10 discipline built on a foundation of high personal standards. This book will show you how to do both.

—Randy Garn
Bestselling Author of *Prosper: Create the Life You Really Want*

THE
DARKSIDE OF DISCIPLINE

STOP CHASING. SUFFER LESS. ACHIEVE MORE.

THE DARKSIDE OF DISCIPLINE

STOP CHASING. SUFFER LESS. ACHIEVE MORE.

CRAIG BALLANTYNE
AND
DANIEL WOODRUM

The Dark Side of Discipline © 2025 Craig Ballantyne.
All rights reserved.

Printed in the United States of America

Published by Igniting Souls
PO Box 43, Powell, OH 43065
IgnitingSouls.com

This book contains material protected under international and federal copyright laws and treaties. Any unauthorized reprint or use of this material is prohibited. No part of this book may be reproduced or transmitted in any form or by any means, electronic or mechanical, including photocopying, recording, or by any information storage and retrieval system, without express written permission from the author.

LCCN: 2025903050
Paperback ISBN: 978-1-63680-472-9
Hardcover ISBN: 978-1-63680-473-6
e-book ISBN: 978-1-63680-474-3

Available in paperback, hardcover, e-book, and audiobook.

Any Internet addresses (websites, blogs, etc.) and telephone numbers printed in this book are offered as a resource. They are not intended in any way to be or imply an endorsement by Igniting Souls, nor does Igniting Souls vouch for the content of these sites and numbers for the life of this book.

Some names and identifying details may have been changed to protect the privacy of individuals.

Dedication

To Brittney, Blease, Banks, and Bellamy—my highest standard, my greatest purpose.
—Daniel Woodrum

To Michelle, Isabella, Sofia, and Jack: Everything for my family.
—Craig Ballantyne

Table of Contents

Introduction xvii

PART I: Stop Chasing

Chapter 1:   The Truth About Discipline: What It Is—
and What It Isn't 3

Chapter 2:   Real Life Discipline: What Successful
People Do and Don't Do 9

Chapter 3:   The Pyramid of Peak Performance:
An Evolution Beyond Discipline 18

Chapter 4:   Building Your Big Why:
Your North Star for Lasting Success 27

Chapter 5:   Specificity: Clarity Breeds Confidence
and Action 34

PART II: Suffer Less

Chapter 6: Effortless Discipline: How to Win without White-Knuckling Your Way Through Life 41

Chapter 7: Exit the Doom Loop: Ending the Cycle of Failure and Frustration 44

Chapter 8: HALT: The Real Reason We Self-Sabotage 49

Chapter 9: The Doom Loop Escape Plan 54

Chapter 10: Systems: Willpower is Weakness, Structure Equals Freedom 57

Chapter 11: Elimination: Subtract the Suffering and Cut the Chaos 65

Chapter 12: Preparation: Grease the Groove and Automate Your Wins 71

Chapter 13: Accountability: Harness the Power of Positive People 76

Chapter 14: Creating Effortless Discipline Systems: Making the Right Decisions Automatic . . . 84

PART III: Achieve More

Chapter 15: The Fastest Path to Freedom and Success . . . 91

Chapter 16: Identity: Who You are is What You Do . . . 94

Chapter 17: The Ultimate Identity Exercise: Reprogram Your Mind for Success 104

Chapter 18: Standards: The Hidden Force that Shapes Your Destiny 108

Chapter 19: Building Your Unbreakable Standards
System: The Final Evolution beyond
Discipline 114

Chapter 20: Beyond Discipline: Stop Chasing.
Suffer Less. Achieve More. 119

Bibliography 123

About the Authors 127

Introduction

Meet Chuck.

On the outside, Chuck had it all.

- Beautiful wife.
- Two adorable kids.
- A fancy red sports car.
- Big biceps and six-pack abs.
- A multi-million dollar business.

But strangers on the internet convinced Chuck that he wasn't successful because he hadn't done their online challenge of random tasks done for a random number of days.

"No, Chuck, you aren't disciplined," they told him, "until you chase *our* definition of discipline."

Chuck took the bait. He spent hours per day dedicated to the program. Getting up at 5:00 a.m. Cold plunging. Reading and exercising twice a day. Posting selfies doing these things.

Chuck finished the challenge. He got his "virtual claps on the back" from people he'd never met and whom he never would meet.

This validation was so strong that Chuck did the challenge again. Shortly after finishing round two (and getting more virtual dopamine hits), Chuck's wife walked out on him, taking the kids.

"You spend half your time doing all that silly stuff," she said, "And the other half with your face glued to your phone for work!"

While learning a powerful lesson, Chuck won the internet but lost the game of life.

Chasing Other People's Definition of Discipline is the Least Disciplined Thing You Can Do

I had always looked up to Chuck because he was a successful entrepreneur, happily married man, and father. I didn't understand his obsession with the challenge. He was already disciplined, a multi-millionaire with six-pack abs, and a leader in his business, family, and community.

Why was he consumed with doing random acts of discipline to impress strangers on the internet? And by extension, why has "doing hard things" become the new "look at me with a Lambo" humblebrag on the internet?

This new obsession with discipline is the wrong path for pursuing what really matters. It is the result of a misalignment of goals and a lack of clearly defined personal identity. Chuck sacrificed his standards, chased someone else's definition of

Introduction

discipline, and lost everything that mattered while impressing no one who did.

In other words, he chucked-up.

Chuck was devastated. I saw a triumphant life turned tragic.

For what?

It turns out Chuck was using the discipline challenge as a way to avoid meeting the real problems of his life head-on, such as working on his marriage.

I see this all the time in our business, coaching clients at my company Early To Rise.

Otherwise smart, hardworking people put a Level 10 effort into Level 1 problems while putting a Level 1 effort into their Level 10 problems.

- Wealthy businessmen make no time for their wives and kids because they are working fourteen hours a day to get even richer.
- Personal trainers with 8 percent body fat and $8 in their bank account spend two hours a day in the gym but no time working on building their business or sales skills, so they stay broke.
- Entrepreneurs create long morning routine rituals while putting off the most important tasks in their business until they are too tired or it's too late in the day.

For many years, I was guilty of making a similar mistake. I used discipline challenges to avoid facing what mattered. I chased "Gold Stars" and virtual claps on the back from strangers.

"Wow, you're so productive; you must be *The World's Most Disciplined Man*," they would say after seeing how much content I created and how many speaking events I did for my business. For years, I felt validated when my clients would

The Darkside of Discipline

refer to me with that title, but the positive recognition provided a slippery slope, putting me in a prison of my design.

I used my obsession with discipline as an excuse to avoid rejection while pursuing what really mattered to me in life—meeting my wife and making time to have a family.

Like Chuck, I nearly threw it all away to the Dark Side of Discipline—putting a Level 10 effort into Level 1 problems while chasing other people's definitions of discipline.

Doubling down on doing hard things was the path of least resistance for me. I built systems that made it easy to live a strict life and work lots of hours.

For years, I chased the Discipline Dragon, piling more and more onto my to-do list.

To be fair, discipline was once my savior—when I was a young, broke, struggling, introverted, socially anxious, binge-drinking personal trainer who suffered from anxiety attacks so badly that I went to the emergency room twice.

In order to beat the booze, I created what I call "Effortless Discipline Systems" to remove myself from toxic environments and social circles, making better decisions and preparing in advance to stay out of trouble.

I also created systems for making time to acquire high-income skills, putting more structure in my day to become more productive, and mastering my mindset to deal with the challenges of entrepreneurship so I could build Early To Rise into a multi-million dollar business.

Discipline even helped me break free from my anxiety and introverted tendencies to become a highly sought-after speaker and business coach.

So yes, "Discipline = Freedom," as Jocko Willink says.

But discipline can also destroy you, and that's what no guru will tell you.

Eventually, discipline became my master, putting me in a prison where I had to adhere to a strict schedule robotically,

Introduction

skip social events, work weekends, and get to bed at 8:00 p.m. so I could wake up at 3:57 a.m. and never miss a workout.

I once had an exercise streak of over one thousand days. I remember doing a bodyweight workout in an airline lounge bathroom in Copenhagen airport. Squats followed by push-ups on the filthy floor. I couldn't miss a day and lose my streak.

I look back and shake my head. My life was as ridiculous as it sounds. What was the point? There are no Gold Medals for working out every day. In fact, this is the Dark Side of Discipline that can destroy you—and your family.

On the bright side, those years spent flirting with the dark side of discipline and living an overly strict and rigid life showed me what was *un*necessary for success.

By now, you're seeing that discipline is a double-edged sword.

You can use discipline to set you free (like it did for me from anxiety and alcohol).

Or you can use discipline to build yourself a prison (like it did for Chuck and the old me when we chased validation from strangers while ignoring what mattered).

Since then, I've escaped the prison that comes from the Dark Side of Discipline.

The solution was an evolution beyond discipline. After building effective systems, I still needed to shift my identity and develop high personal standards that served me—rather than me serving them. Standards leverage the positive power of discipline— making the right decisions automatic for success—without dragging you down to the dark side.

I used the systems and standards you'll learn about in this book to build "level 10 discipline" where it mattered in my life. This has helped me to do everything from overcoming crippling anxiety to meeting my wife and raising three kids under the age of three, all while building multiple businesses and writing best-selling books (and to keep my unnecessary-but-nice-to-have six-pack abs at the age of forty-nine).

If you want to stop white-knuckling your way through life, gritting your teeth, and praying that your willpower will hold out for another hour to get you through the day, then you need to evolve beyond fleeting daily motivation and short-term challenges.

Discipline can set you free in the short term, but only through the setting of high personal standards can you remain free for life. As we teach our clients:

Standards Eat Discipline For Breakfast

My clients have used these systems and standards in this book to double their businesses, write best-selling books, and even get remarried to ex-wives.

You've probably noticed this book is short. That's because success is simple. You don't need pages of statistics and complex solutions to change your life.

You need to know what matters.

You need simple systems to eliminate what doesn't.

And you need to set higher standards to achieve what does.

That's it.

There are three phases to your evolution and journey to freedom that you'll discover in this book.

1. The first step is to build Effortless Discipline Systems. Systems are a series of organized processes that deliver predictable and sustainable results.
2. The second step is to create a strong, unshakeable identity. Identity is the set of personal traits and beliefs that characterize you.

Introduction

3. The third step is where we help you establish high personal standards that make success automatic. Standards are frameworks for your thoughts and behaviors. They are your personal code for determining what's acceptable to you and prevent you from compromising on what matters.

This evolution is exactly what a high performer—who wants it all—needs in life.

My co-author, Daniel Woodrum, and I have been obsessed with discipline, productivity, and transformation for over twenty-five years. This book is our life's work.

We've spent decades coaching people to get fit, get rich, change their lives, and improve their marriages. In our business, Early to Rise, we've helped over one million people achieve their dreams, grow their businesses, become uber-productive, and lose weight without sacrificing family time or their social lives.

We've been around the block and know how systems and standards can transform people's lives, but we've also seen how the unnecessary pursuit of other people's definitions of discipline destroys dreams.

We wrote this book so that you can achieve your biggest goals without the unnecessary suffering so many approaches to discipline and common motivational challenges bring.

Along the way, you'll discover:

- The one "North Star" decision required for achieving results faster and getting back on track whenever extreme obstacles get in your way.
- How to quickly and easily shift your identity—a key element of high performance—so you can replace bad habits practically overnight.

- A formula for creating your own personal standards of excellence that deliver *your* dream life without extreme sacrifices or suffering.

You'll also be shown what doesn't work and is not necessary—saving you hundreds of hours that most people spend chasing the wrong path to success—this might even save your marriage like it could have done for Chuck (and did for Marcus Martinez, whom you'll meet in a moment).

This book is the fastest path you'll find to automating success. We'll show you simple yet powerful strategies for doing what you should do, when you should do it, no matter how you feel about doing it. You'll soon be applying a Level 10 effort to your Level 10 problems automatically—because that's what a person like you, with high personal standards, does.

With your new systems, identity, and a higher set of standards, you'll become unstoppable in every area of life—from the boardroom to the living room.

We've created a series of tools to accompany this book. To accelerate your results, download them for free now at DarkSideofDiscipline.com/success or scan this QR code.

PART 1
Stop Chasing

1

The Truth About Discipline: What It Is—and What It Isn't

> Following the crowd is not a winning approach to life.
> —*Tim Tebow*

Everything you know about discipline is wrong.
 Discipline is *not* joining the 5 AM Club, ultramarathoning, intermittent fasting, exercising twice per day, reading a book per week, or living with a Navy SEAL.
 Discipline is *not* found at the bottom of an ice bath.
 Discipline is *not* about chasing another person's dreams.
 Discipline is *not* checking every box beside a laundry list of "hard" tasks.

Discipline is *not* about enduring more pain than the person beside you at CrossFit.

Discipline is also *not* "one size fits all." It is not a transferrable trait. Just because you are world-class disciplined in one area of life doesn't mean you will be disciplined in working on your marriage (Exhibit A: Tiger Woods).

To find true discipline, you have to back up.

First, you must figure out what matters in your life. We call this identifying your values and vision. And then, you have to do the hardest work of all—thinking—to build out a custom blueprint for *your* future, not comparing your habits to someone else and chasing *their* definition of success.

When you know your values and vision, you start to make better decisions.

Because even good habits can put you in a bad place when you're misaligned about what really matters.

Is it good to exercise? Yes.

Is it good for a busy parent to exercise twice a day every day—because an online challenge demands it—even if that means missing out on family time? No.

Whether it's two-hour morning routines or ninety-day challenges of nineteen tasks, many people are doing more (and suffering more) but achieving less on what matters.

Have you ever noticed that none of these online discipline challenges ever include "spend thirty minutes with your spouse" or "an hour with your kids"?

And we wonder why more and more people are busier than ever but more disconnected from their families and real-world communities.

That's why chasing other people's definitions of discipline is the least disciplined thing you can do.

So... What Is Discipline?

When you were a child, you learned about discipline from a teacher or parent. That definition of discipline—using punishment to correct disobedience—is not where we want to focus. However, many of us confuse that definition with the discipline we can use to improve our lives.

High-performer discipline is not about punishment, suffering, or correcting disobedience. You don't need to punish yourself to improve your life.

Let me repeat that:

You don't need to punish yourself to improve your life.

Unfortunately, many people have these two definitions blended together, thinking, "If I want to be successful, I have to suffer." No, that's not it at all.

If you want to be successful, you need to identify what's most important to you, create a plan to achieve it, and build the systems to stick to it without getting distracted.

If you want to know whether you are disciplined, take this easy test.

Step 1: Identify Your *Real* Problems

- Write down the three most significant problems in your life that are holding you back right now.
- Be brutally honest—what areas are causing the most stress, frustration, or failure?
(Examples: Struggling marriage, poor health, business not growing, money issues, addictions, vices, etc.)

Step 2: Measure Your Effort

- Next to each problem, rate your effort to fix it on a scale from 1–10.
- A 10/10 means you are all in, fully committed, and taking daily action to fix the problem.
- A 1/10 means you are ignoring it or procrastinating on it and hoping it gets better on its own.
- If this sounds like you, you're a Struggler.

Step 3: Identify Where You're Wasting Energy

- Write down anything where you're putting a Level 10 effort into something that is *not* a Level 10 problem.
- Be honest: Are you spending hours on a long, unnecessary morning routine, working out twice a day (even though you're already fit), or learning a new skill while avoiding your critical real-life issues?
- If so, you're a Wild Horse—running fast but in the wrong direction.

Strugglers → You're putting a Level 1 effort into Level 10 problems. You know exactly what you need to fix—your marriage, your finances, your business—but you keep putting it off, convincing yourself that you don't know where to start.

Wild Horses → You're putting a Level 10 effort into Level 1 problems—your 2-hour morning routine, starting a podcast and a YouTube channel, reading five books a month—while avoiding the hard work that would actually change your life.

It's time to flip the script. Start TODAY by committing to put Level 10 effort into the problems that truly matter. That's the genuine definition of discipline.

The Truth About Discipline: What It Is—and What It Isn't

> The Ultimate Definition of Discipline means putting a Level 10 effort into your Level 10 problem in life.
> —Craig Ballantyne

This definition is a secret to success. If you learn nothing else from this book—in fact, if you stop reading this book right now—this definition of discipline would be life-changing for you.

Of course, I encourage you to keep reading so you build the systems and standards to do this, but this shift in alignment is all you need to finally have the breakthroughs you've been seeking—and failing to find—in online challenges, motivational seminars, and other habit change books.

Anything below a Level 10 effort into your Level 10 problems means you are not as disciplined as you need to be. It doesn't matter how many cold plunges you do at 5:00 a.m. while reading your book of the week. If you aren't putting a Level 10 effort into your Level 10 problems, it means you are procrastinating and avoiding what really matters. That is undisciplined.

Discipline is not doing "hard things" as defined by others. Discipline is having systems and standards that guarantee you tackle your Level 10 problems in life and move you toward your goals while destroying the bad habits that hold you back.

In our twenty-five-plus years of helping people transform their lives, we've discovered one harsh fact. Most people find it easier to start something new rather than tackle the big problems that exist in their lives right now. That's because it is more rewarding to put a Level 5 effort into a Level 2 problem. You immediately get a dopamine hit for taking easy action (such as signing up for an online challenge).

> **Most people find it easier to start something new rather than tackle the big problems that exist in their lives right now. That's because it's more rewarding to put a Level 5 effort into a Level 2 problem.**

It's much harder to push through a Level 10 problem because of the effort that is required and the low reward you are likely to get each day. It's easy to start a new diet and lose that first pound, but exponentially harder to lose the last pound. It's easy to start writing a book, but it's much harder to finish a tenth rewrite and round of editing. And it's easier to put up a dating profile and get dopamine hits from online flirting than it is to fix your marriage of fifteen years.

But discipline—putting a Level 10 effort into your Level 10 problem—is what separates the winners in life from those who always feel like they are struggling or bouncing like a ping-pong ball from one idea to the next. If you feel like you're on the verge of success but can't figure out why you can't break through, shifting your definition of discipline to our definition is the missing link.

All that matters in life is doing the work on what really matters. Everything else is just entertainment.

The Discipline Scorecard

How does your discipline rate? Want to know? We've created a simple discipline scorecard. This quick self-assessment also shows you what you need to do to get to the next level. Download it for free now at DarkSideofDiscipline.com/success or scan the QR code below.

2

Real Life Discipline: What Successful People Do and Don't Do

Meet Marcus, "The Anti-Chuck."
When I first met Marcus Martinez, he was living Chuck's nightmare.

Working too much and neglecting his family led him to divorce. Marcus had become "that single dad" with weekend visitation rights to his three kids.

When he joined our coaching program at Early to Rise, Marcus admitted that he had made his fair share of mistakes leading to his broken marriage.

The Darkside of Discipline

He was a road warrior, traveling for work nearly every week. Work trips often included drinking and late nights. This resulted in fatigue and week-long illnesses upon getting home, and that meant not being a great partner or father when it mattered. It was an undisciplined doom loop that he couldn't continue. Marcus knew things had to change.

Unlike most people, Marcus didn't run from his Level 10 problem in life, nor did he chase someone else's definition of discipline. Instead, he made the effort to identify what mattered to him. He ignored everyone else's goals, committed to his journey, and dedicated himself with ruthless and relentless persistence, and consistency.

It wasn't easy, but we built effortless discipline systems and boundaries for Marcus that made it simple for Marcus to put a Level 10 effort into his Level 10 problems. We transformed his identity, tossed the toxic temptations, and destroyed his distractions through the elevation of his personal standards.

When Marcus created his values and vision—using the information in the next section of the book—he had the power to make better daily decisions. Doing the right thing was effortless and automatic and didn't rely on exhausting the limited amount of willpower we all have. His business grew, he had more freedom, and his ex-wife began to notice.

Over a twelve-month period, where Marcus developed his Level 10 discipline, he began showing up unselfishly. And that's when something clicked.

First, his ex-wife was grateful. Her gratitude turned to friendship. The next thing you know, they were dating again. Discipline eventually led to a miracle—remarriage.

Recently, Marcus and his ex-wife/new wife celebrated the arrival of their fourth child.

Marcus jokes that his friends refer to him as the only man who's been "to the other side and back."

Against all odds. No cold plunges required. No Navy SEALS yelling in his face. Marcus achieved the ultimate success simply by knowing what mattered and raising his personal standards to achieve it.

The foundation was set through Marcus chasing no one else's best life but his own. He did the work, created his vision, and worked the systems you'll get in this book.

Marcus ran his own race. And when you run yours, you're guaranteed to win.

How This Book Is Set Up

I'm not a fan of books where the author takes the easy way out and says, "Don't read this book from start to finish. Instead, jump around and find what is useful for you."

A book isn't a garage sale. It's not your job, as the reader, to do the work of searching for gold nuggets. That's why I've created *The Dark Side of Discipline* as a logical, step-by-step discipline download.

Who This Book Is For

It's not just for the "Chucks" of the world who are already disciplined and want to go to the next level. It's also for the beginners who need to break bad habits, the busy parents with demanding careers, and those with incredible ambitions who need the extra edge to achieve a big breakthrough. I call these groups of people the sabotaged strugglers, the awakened ambitious, the passionate ones, and the relapsers.

The Sabotaged Strugglers

You're stuck with a bad habit you just can't shake. For the past few months or years (or your entire life), you've been struggling to "have discipline." This comes through in life as being overweight, drinking too much, or not getting up on time.

I get it. I've been there. I've had just about every bad habit and been undisciplined in every way you can imagine:

- binge-eating
- binge-drinking
- binge-watching
- binge-video gaming

And that's why I had to build systems that allowed me to make the right actions automatic in my life for success. These systems worked so well that people called me the world's most disciplined man. I then taught these same systems to millions of people through my online fitness business so they could lose weight for life, and tens of thousands of people are looking to become more productive through my books.

I've used these systems to stop drinking, quit swearing, get in shape, overcome the fear of rejection, and go from a boring, robotic speaker to a dynamic, confident speaker on stage and in videos. Once you define your discipline, you'll discover how to build systems that set you free from what holds you back.

With Effortless Discipline Systems, you'll struggle no more.

The Awakened Ambitious

I once attended a seminar with a motivational guru and his "cult." At one point, an audience member (a.k.a. "cult member") asked the guru to give him a beat down. Literally, he asked the guru to physically beat the bad habits out of him.

To my surprise, the guru did exactly that. I looked around the room, thinking, "Someone else must think this is crazy." Nope. Everyone cheered it on. I couldn't believe it.

Real Life Discipline: What Successful People Do and Don't Do

But that's not me. I'm just like you. Normal.

And so, when we look around and see all these people jumping into frozen lakes or doing ultramarathons just to prove they are disciplined, we don't understand. We think, "The Discipline Emperor has no clothes." You know that sitting in a cold tub of water does not directly translate to success in life.

But social media might have put doubts in your mind. You find yourself thinking, "Wait a minute…maybe I should start cold-plunging at 4:00 a.m. after five hours of sleep. Maybe that's the secret!"

How did people in the 1880s and 1980s ever become successful without cold plunges, long workouts, biohacking, listening to podcasts, or knowing the universe had their back?

Maybe because none of these are necessary or sufficient for success.

The good news is that if you step back and do a quick reality check, you'll realize many successful people did not or do not use cold showers or other life hacks as part of their success systems:

- Taylor Swift—*Time* Magazine's 2023 Person of the Year
- Elon Musk—2024 Richest Person on Earth
- Martin Luther King Jr.
- John F. Kennedy
- Warren Buffett
- Oprah

The list is long and proves that a laundry list of discipline tasks and the latest trends is neither necessary nor sufficient for success.

On the other hand, doing the work on what matters in life is what will get you the results you want. The ultimate life hack is putting a Level 10 effort into your Level 10 problem. Sure, the work you do might not go viral on social media, but it will actually lead to results with less chasing and suffering.

The Passionate Ones

Ah, my wild horses. I love this group.

You know the old saying, "You can lead a horse to water, but you can't make them drink?" The passionate ones are the wild horses that chug all the water, snort all the oats, and sprint off in a frenzy, looking for more, only to exhaust themselves in the search.

Each day, social media provides you with another disciplinary distraction you want to add to your list.

- Your "dues" aren't paid unless you do 100 daily pushups? Game on!
- Your diet isn't manly unless you eat bull testicles like the Liver King? Bottoms up!
- You're not disciplined unless you hit the three-minute mark in a freezing-cold ice bath? Hold my beer! (Better yet, take it in the cold plunge with you!)

Pretty soon, you're like the albino monk in Dan Brown's *The Da Vinci Code*, self-flagellating yourself before bed every night.

Stop. Just stop.

I need you to pull back and do something harder than another physical challenge. I need you to stop suffering.

"For some people, doing all these things can just be a continuation of a trauma pattern in their life," a friend told me. "Always having to take their 'suffering' to another level and to follow the crowd. But there's no substitute for awareness and getting to the root of why you're making the choices you're making and asking if they're truly serving you."

This book will teach you how to think, how to orient yourself in the right direction, and how to make sure that your ambition doesn't cause more problems—as it did for Chuck.

The Relapsers

"Craig, I'm doing another discipline program, and it's been really helpful," one of my clients said.

A multi-millionaire in the tech industry, he works a thirteen-hour day. He battles addiction. He repeatedly makes promises he doesn't keep. He's done multiple discipline challenges, and none have made these destructive bad habits disappear. In fact, they often grew worse between challenges when he rebounded into self-sabotaging behavior.

And yet, somehow, he's convinced the "challenges" have been helpful.

Based on my experience, completing a "discipline" challenge guarantees nothing. In fact, many people often relapse.

Even in my original business, Turbulence Training, where we held twelve-week transformation contests that helped tens of thousands of busy men and women lose weight, we saw a greater than 30 percent relapse rate in regaining the weight after our challenges.

A challenge shows you what you are capable of, but it provides artificial boundaries, fleeting growth, and little development. Once it's over, you're on your own, often with no plan, less willpower, and without the benefits of positive people, and you soon return to old, negative ways.

The lifelong success solution is deeper than a set of discipline tasks done daily.

Stop chasing and start running your own race.

Meet the Real World's Most Disciplined Man

Did you know that the Most Disciplined Man in the World

- never exercised
- would laugh at the idea of a cold plunge
- liked to eat an entire box of peanut brittle in one sitting

He would be mocked by the hardcore gurus of discipline today.

Yet, his personal definition of discipline allowed him to overcome the tragedy of his nine-year-old son dying from leukemia and himself going blind in one eye. He even had the discipline to learn braille after being told he might lose the other eye. His discipline turned him into a billionaire who lived to ninety-nine years old (just thirty-four days shy of one hundred).

He was the man who

- mentored one of the richest men on the planet
- turned tens of thousands of people into millionaires
- inspired billions of people with his wisdom

His name was Charlie Munger.

And I will argue he was the world's most disciplined man. He had everything a man could want in life: family, health, wealth, prestige, and even power. Because he had a personal definition of discipline, he knew what mattered, and he had the discipline to spend all his time on it and didn't waste his life chasing other people's definitions of discipline that would hinder his success.

> "The only real test of intelligence is if you get what you want out of life," said Naval Ravikant, a famous and wealthy Silicon Valley investor.
>
> We believe you can replace the word "intelligence" with "discipline," and the quote would be just as true.

3

The Pyramid of Peak Performance: An Evolution Beyond Discipline

> The challenge never ends. The finish line keeps moving.
> I'm not telling you not to take the challenge. I'm telling
> you the real challenge starts after you finish.
> —*Tim S. Grover*

If you're constantly feeling like you're falling short despite doing discipline challenges— where you get short-term whipped into conformity but lack long-term change in what matters—the missing link from your life is setting higher personal standards and putting a Level 10 effort into your Level 10 problem.

Now, I know what you're thinking, "But how do I do that?"

I want to introduce you to the Pyramid of Peak Performance, designed by my co-author, Daniel Woodrum.

The Pyramid of Peak Performance is your roadmap to success. It aligns your actions, automates discipline, and elevates your standards—without relying on fleeting motivation or white-knuckling through life.

It also relies on one thing. Get this wrong, and you'll be chasing the Discipline Dragon forever or putting yourself in prison.

That one thing is knowing your Big Why—what matters to you—and deciding to pursue it over whatever latest trend everyone else is pursuing.

Get this right; you'll achieve your dream life. Get this wrong, and it could destroy you.

THE PYRAMID OF PEAK PERFORMANCE

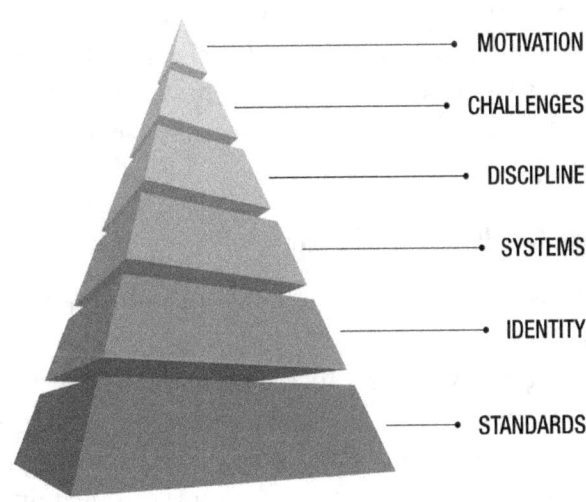

The Pyramid of Peak Performance

The **Pyramid of Peak Performance** is a structured framework that ensures sustainable success by building each layer on a solid foundation. Follow along to learn how to align your actions, automate success, and elevate your standards.

Motivation—The Spark

We put motivation at the top of the pyramid because you can look at it as the icing on the cake. It can help you kickstart action or reignite your momentum, but motivation on its own can never make for lifelong change. It's unreliable, unsustainable, and collapses under pressure.

"People often say that motivation doesn't last. Well, neither does bathing—that's why we recommend it daily," said Zig Ziglar, one of the most famous motivational speakers of the twentieth century.

You are welcome to—after putting a Level 10 effort into your Level 10 problem—watch your favorite motivational YouTube video every day. But please realize motivation doesn't guarantee consistent action (like systems) or the ability to automatically make the right decisions (like standards).

Motivation is like a match—it lights the fire, but it burns out quickly. Discipline and systems are the fuel that keeps the fire burning.

Challenges—The Double-Edged Sword

We'd like to pause and honor our enemy—the Discipline Challenge.

Challenges are almost always a random list of things to do with arbitrary rules. They often focus on proving something to others for no good reason. On the bright side, challenges provide instant gratification (i.e., dopamine hits), social validation, and a clear start and finish for inspiration. The dark side of challenges is that they are one-size-fits-all, unsustainable, and put you on the path to chasing the wrong goals.

Real success comes from focusing on what matters to you.

The number one benefit of doing any one of the many online challenges is that it throws a drowning man a lifeline.

A few years ago, I criticized a popular online challenge in a social media video. My Instagram inbox was flooded with people's messages on both sides. Some people thanked me for calling out the dark side of the challenge. But an equal, although much more passionate, group of enraged advocates pushed back.

I noticed one commonality in the advocates that I had never considered before. Each one of them told a story about how the challenge saved them from the lowest of their lows—alcoholism, drugs, and severe obesity. It was an aha moment.

I still don't believe a hardcore challenge is the fastest way from point A to point B; however, it can be an effective way to save a drowning person.

For someone in their darkest moments, success in a discipline challenge provides light.

I built my first career on a similar premise. My Turbulence Training 12-Week Transformation Contest helped thousands of men and women like Todd Arnold from Wisconsin go from 400 pounds to 350 pounds in twelve weeks and eventually all the way down to a life-saving 200 pounds.

But for most of us who are not addicted to drugs or alcohol or food and who are just looking for an edge to go to the next level in every area of life… challenges are *not* the right choice. There is a faster way to get from where you are now to where you want to be. It doesn't require suffering, doing hard things, or spending hours per day on tasks unrelated to your big goals in life.

The Darkside of Discipline

Let me explain using an extreme analogy.

If you chopped your finger off in the kitchen, would you trek barefoot through the snow to a hospital—or drive? The answer is obvious. Yet, when it comes to fixing real problems in life, we often choose suffering over solutions.

Why, when you have a specific problem in your life, such as troubles in your marriage, would you turn to a general discipline challenge that takes a long time rather than acutely attacking your real problem immediately?

Why do nineteen things to build general discipline when doing just one thing—putting a Level 10 effort into your Level 10 problem—is enough? The answer is procrastination, of course. It's easier to start a bunch of new things than it is to solve the most difficult problem in your life.

But back to honoring "the challenge."

What are all the things that discipline challenges and transformation contests do right?

- Starting point and direction
- "Dopamine Hits" from checking things off
- Day 1 Momentum
- Mid-point Motivation
- End Is Near Relief
- Social Support
- General Confidence

But is a "100 Pushups in 100 Days" challenge the only place you can get these things? Of course not. You can get these things anywhere, anytime. Discipline is not about adding more items to your already overwhelming to-do list.

Discipline challenges also violate the well-known 80-20, or Pareto, principle. Eighty percent of your results come from 20 percent of your efforts. That's why well-built, effortless discipline systems (that you'll learn below) deliver far more discipline in every area of life than doing a challenge of twenty different activities that cause unnecessary stress and suffering.

Stop chasing. There is a better way, a smarter way, to fix your problems. And that's good news because it means you can become disciplined faster, with less suffering, when you do it the "Effortless Discipline Way."

Plus, you avoid the dangerous detour of the Dark Side of Discipline that destroyed Chuck's life, and you avoid the risk of having a huge setback from something that was meant to be a positive force in your life.

The online challenge can nudge you in the right direction—or push you off a cliff into a deadly direction.

Choose wisely.

Discipline

Discipline is execution. But without systems, it's exhausting. The key to lasting success isn't grinding harder—it's designing your life so the right actions happen automatically. Discipline is what persists even when motivation wavers.

But if you rely on discipline without systems—which most people would refer to as willpower—it's not a long-term or reliable solution. Eventually, long days wear you down. People can break, but systems won't.

We feel we've made our case on discipline already. Now, let's talk about building the foundation underneath it so discipline serves you rather than the other way around.

Systems

As I'm sure an ancient philosopher once said, "Give a man a challenge, you make him disciplined for a few days but teach a man to create systems, you give him effortless discipline for a lifetime."

Systems are the glue that holds discipline together, bridging the gap between intention and action. They create structure and reduce decision fatigue so the right actions become automatic.

Systems help you do the boring but essential work, such as getting to bed on time, building bulletproof morning routines, destroying distractions, and tossing toxic temptations.

We're here to teach you everything you need to know about building effortless discipline systems that will set you free of bad habits and put you on the fast track to success with good habits.

You'll never need another challenge, another contest, another "short-term sprint" followed by a rebound doom loop cycle of bad behaviors.

You will forever be a high performer with these systems on your side.

Identity

Identity is who you become as the result of the systems and habits you've created. This layer is key because it influences your actions on a fundamental level; your habits are most likely to align with who you believe you are.

When you genuinely believe that you are someone who keeps commitments, for example, your actions automatically follow suit. Individuals who see themselves as "organized" will naturally follow systems that reinforce this identity.

For example, if you shift your identity to "I'm the type of person who takes control of my mornings," supportive behavior becomes easier for you to do. Going to bed on time, getting up with your alarm, and planning and preparing for your morning work are natural extensions of this identity. When your actions align with this new identity, waking up early becomes effortless and is your standard.

Standards

If you don't set a baseline standard for what you'll accept in your life, you'll find it's easy to slip into behaviors and attitudes or a quality of life that's far below what you deserve.

> You need to set and live by these standards no matter what happens in your life.
> —*Tony Robbins,* Awaken the Giant Within: How to Take Immediate Control of Your Mental, Emotional, Physical and Financial Destiny!

Standards are the non-negotiable code (rules, operating systems) for how you live your life. They are the foundation of long-term behavior change and achieving peak performance. Show me your standards, and I'll show you your future.

Your standards do not change because of stress, peer pressure, mood, criticism, environment, or temptations.

Violating your standards is the worst thing you can do for your confidence, your integrity, alignment, your relationships with your spouse, your children, and God.

Standards Eat Discipline for Breakfast

Take two people.
One a vegan; one a normal eater.
Put them in a room with no food for 12 hours.
Then, put a cheeseburger in front of them.
The vegan won't crack because they have standards.
The other person won't last long because willpower doesn't work forever.
Standards eat discipline for breakfast (and lunch).

The Darkside of Discipline

Standards set me free—quicker and easier than discipline.

"Chasing more discipline" is the white-knuckling, grit your teeth, grind it out, deplete your willpower way to get through life. It's exhausting and, worse, rarely effective in the long term.

Raising your standards is harder at first—it forces you to think instead of react. But once you do, success becomes automatic. You won't need to "push through"—your standards will pull you forward.

Standards require self-reflection and introspection, but if you give us just a few minutes in guided exercises found in this book, you'll have set the stage for the biggest breakthroughs in your life simply by raising your standards. In less than ten minutes of thinking, you can make greater life-changing progress than in ten weeks of cold plunging.

Setting higher personal standards helped me quit swearing, procrastinating, porn, and booze. There's no downside to setting—and sticking to—higher standards.

> Standards eat discipline for breakfast.
> —Craig Ballantyne

4

Building Your Big Why: Your North Star for Lasting Success

> Make a plan that truly reflects your goals and interests, and you'll be more likely to execute.
> —*Tim S. Grover*, Relentless: From Good to Great to Unstoppable

In April 2003, Aron Ralston set out for a hike in Canyonlands National Park, Utah. As he descended into the canyon, he dislodged a large boulder. The massive rock smashed into him and trapped his right arm between it and the canyon wall. Aron was stuck. He had told no one where he was going, and there was no one else for miles around.

You may have heard about Aron. He's the guy who sawed off his arm with a dull two-inch knife to survive. Hollywood made a movie about him, *127 Hours.*

"Not Dying" is a pretty effective Big Why that will make you move mountains in your life (even if you can't move a boulder). Likewise, the first step in developing discipline for lifelong habit change and setting high standards, or allowing you to do the seemingly impossible in anything, is having a Big Why that matters. Your Big Why gives you the energy, focus, and discipline to escape the compound of complacency, where your dreams and discipline might otherwise go to die.

I knew that I could not live my dream life if I remained a binge drinker. I did not deserve an amazing woman like my wife Michelle, nor could I be a great family man and father. Though we had yet to meet, the idea of Michelle was the Big Why behind my ability to kick booze to the curb—and I was the reason she quit too.

Today, I continue to harness the power of my Big Why to give me discipline to fight off complacency.

On my phone, I have a note that simply says:

Everything for my family.

This is my Big Why.

- Don't want to get up at 2:30 a.m. to feed my six-month-old and then stay up to finish this book so I can be done with my real work when the kids get up at six? Too bad. Everything for my family.
- Don't want to cut back on my workouts and go to the gym only three times per week for thirty minutes because I need more time at home to help my wife

with our three kids (under the age of three)? Too bad. Everything for my family.
- Don't want to lug two cribs, three strollers, four suitcases, fifty stuffed animals, and six hundred diapers onto a Spirit Airlines flight to Orlando so we can visit Disney World? Too bad. Everything for my family!

Your Big Why supports your Values and Vision and dictates every daily decision. It keeps you on a straight line to success.

There's nothing more powerful for making you more disciplined than knowing what matters and knowing what does not.

> Discipline = Devotion to Your Vision + the Right Daily Decisions

---

How a "Big Why" Convinced My Wife to Quit Drinking During COVID-19
By Michelle Kavanagh

> *My wife Michelle gave up alcohol during a time when many people started drinking more. Here's how she did it without joining any challenges.*
> *—Craig Ballantyne*

I quit drinking in March 2020 because I was using alcohol as a way to escape like most people do. I didn't want to deal with real, complicated things going on. I'd rather numb the feelings and dance the night away. I had just met Craig and could tell that he was seriously someone with whom I could see myself for a long time.

> I didn't want to mess it up. I was not a casual drinker. I liked gin and tequila (just not together!). After a few nights out with friends, I decided this was not the future I wanted. This was something I had been doing for years, and it didn't leave me feeling complete. So, that day, I decided to quit.
>
> And I've never looked back. I decided to do the hard inner work and ask the deep questions. Now, I am truly the happiest and most fulfilled because I made that one decision and everything else in my life started to get better.
>
> If you are on the fence—do it! Sober living is the new cool!

In our coaching program at Early To Rise, I take our clients through a series of short mental exercises to get their values and vision out of their heads.

Your values are your core goals and desires that are unlikely to change over the years. For example, by your early twenties, you probably knew you wanted to get married, have kids, start a business, and grow your family's wealth so that you could give them a life of luxury and travel that you might not have had as a kid. It's unlikely those values would change at age thirty, forty, or fifty. The only difference is you might have added grandkids to your hopes and dreams.

Your vision is a more specific description of what you want to achieve in a specific time frame. For example, when I hired my first business coach, his first question on our initial call was, "What do you want your business to look like in five years?"

My reply was, "I want to own a business like EarlyToRise.com." (Early to Rise was owned by a gentleman named Mark Ford at the time.) After creating a plan with my coach to pursue my vision, I earned the right to buy Early To Rise five years, three months, and seventeen days later.

The power of your Values and Vision is that they set a North Star for your life. They are, as I describe them to my clients, the "treasure map" for your life. They are a movie script for your future that, when written out, should be so clear and visual that anyone reading your vision can feel like they are watching a movie. Your values and vision keep you on the straight line to success and help you avoid interesting yet dangerous detours (like doing discipline challenges that lead to divorce).

When you have created your values and vision, your every decision is made from a place of customization. Your goals and dreams are clear. You stop chasing other people's definitions of discipline. You stop doing "hard things" for the sake of impressing strangers on the internet, and you only do the right things that take you closer to your big goals and dreams. Essentially, you run your own race in life, the opinions of others be damned. This is what separates people who are fulfilled in life from those who are always chasing the Discipline Dragon, looking for a dopamine hit from starting some new challenge or pursuit that doesn't actually matter to their dreams and often leads to destruction.

It's your life. You can do anything, but you can't do everything. Choose wisely.

You can do anything, but you can't do everything. Choose wisely.

These tools are so important to your success that I want to share them here with you.

1. First, create your Big Why statement.

   Why do you want to be more disciplined?

   My Big Why: "Everything for my family."

Yours might be:

- "To become the ultimate version of myself."
- "To lift my family out of generational curses."
- "To live a life of integrity with my relationship with God."
- "To get rich and leave my family with generational wealth."

You'll get no judgment from us on your Big Why. Make the statement that matters to you.

2. Do the Vision exercise, creating a three-year Vision for Your Life. Write the vision statement as if you were writing from the future, and you have already accomplished the big goals in your vision.

The Vision exercise might be new for readers, so I've created a short free video with more explanation on how to create your vision. You'll also get access to download the worksheets and see my answers to guide you in creating yours.

Just visit DarkSideOfDiscipline.com/success or scan the QR code for access.

PERFECT LIFE VISION

The date is: _____

Location: _____

I am with: _____

We are celebrating: _____

In the past three years we have:

Big Accomplishment #1: _____

Big Accomplishment #2: _____

Big Accomplishment #3: _____

Every year I do / Our family does this: _____

My partner and I do this: _____

What is the biggest obstacle to achieving this vision?: _____

What is the 1st step towards overcoming it?: _____

The Perfect Life Vision worksheet.

5

Specificity: Clarity Breeds Confidence and Action

> First say to yourself what you would be,
> and then do what you have to do.
> —*Epictetus*

Haruki Murakami is a novelist. He wakes up every morning at 4:00 a.m. and writes until 9:00 a.m. He goes to bed at 9:00 p.m. When he was younger, he smoked, drank, and stayed out late. Today, he does not vary his routine. His social calendar has suffered at the expense of his strict routine, but Murakami focuses on the relationship with his readers and his work. His priority, he says, is to write better books, not to be a social butterfly.

Specificity: Clarity Breeds Confidence and Action

Like Murakami, you need to run your own race.

If you start out chasing someone else's finish line, you'll lose every time. Setting out with the wrong goal in mind is just as bad as not setting out at all. And if you start going faster or getting "more disciplined," it doesn't help. In fact, it can set you off course even faster.

The idea of running your own race when pursuing your goals and your definition of discipline may be one of the most important success ideas.

"It's also one of the hardest things to do," says Matt Smith, one of my earliest mentors and former business partners at EarlyToRise.com. "For most of the race, everyone, including you, thinks you may be making a big mistake. But once you've done it, it's easy. You realize the social signals are all inverted. If everyone approves, you're doing it wrong."

The two biggest directional errors people make with discipline are:

1. Chasing other people's definition of discipline.
2. Being vague.

In twenty-seven years as a personal trainer, business coach, and millionaire mentor, I've heard thousands of people share vague, general goals with me. They fail almost 100 percent of the time.

- "I want to get rich."
- "I want to lose weight."
- "I want to have an impact."
- "I want to have more discipline."

What do these statements even mean? It could be anything. And if it could be anything, that means it's impossible to build the right plan.

The solution?

You must have a specific definition of success.

Before you can achieve something, you must define it. We can't build you a step-by-step treasure map until you tell me *exactly* what you want to find.

How can you identify exactly what you want? Be clear. Be concise. Clarity is key. Tell me what you want to achieve and why.

Why Do You Want to Be Disciplined at All?

Here are a few questions that most discipline challengers never ask in the first place.

- Why do I want to be disciplined?
- What does "discipline" really mean to me?
- What specific result do I want to achieve from being "more disciplined"?
- How can I build the right type of discipline that gets me this specific result as fast as possible with as little suffering as possible?

The reason why people don't ask these questions is because thinking is the hardest discipline of all!

It's much easier to start a new project designed by someone else that helps us procrastinate on taking control of our own lives.

But deep down, the real reasons we want to become disciplined are because we equate discipline with success, with eliminating bad habits that make us feel out of sorts, and because it is a virtuous quality, which is the basis of a happy and fulfilled life.

How do we become disciplined in a way that will give us the life we want?

Specificity: Clarity Breeds Confidence and Action

For example, I wanted to write a 25,000-word book that shows readers the fastest, most effective way to achieve discipline and success in their lives.

Once I started writing the book, I shared the deadline date for my first draft with my top coaching clients so they could hold me accountable to follow through.

To achieve my specific definition of success, I first had to write one thousand words per day, which I struggled with some mornings until my Big Why and public accountability kicked in. Then, I had to spend a couple of weeks editing "the slop" down to something more presentable and professional before the deadline.

You need a specific definition of success for every goal in life, from your health goals to your wealth goals, and you even need a precise definition of what you hope to achieve from reading this book.

And, never forget, you must not chase other people's definitions of discipline because that alone can destroy you. Your goal is not to go with the flow but to create your own flow.

Becoming disciplined—in a way that actually improves your life—begins with correctly deciding what you want to achieve.

If you miss this step, like Chuck did, you will make things worse.

So, I ask you, What exactly do you want to achieve concerning discipline and why?

- Do you want to start exercising for thirty minutes a day, four days per week, so that you lose ten pounds in ninety days and reduce your scary blood lipid levels down to a specific healthy range?
- Do you want to stop watching Netflix on work nights so that you finally get to bed on time and, thus, get up on time without hitting snooze in the morning?

- Do you want to overcome your camera-shyness and start making five videos per week to promote your business so you no longer rely only on word-of-mouth to get clients?
- Do you want to stop working past 7:00 p.m. or stop checking your phone when you're with your kids?
- Do you want to fix your marriage and have more date nights with your spouse?

The 30-Second Clarity Exercise

To find clarity, take thirty seconds to answer the questions below:

- What specifically do you want to stop doing? Why?
- What specifically do you want to start doing? Why?

You must have the answers to these questions before you begin your pursuit of discipline. You cannot be confused or have doubts or uncertainty.

Clarity is the key.

Clarity allows you to say *no* to the wrong things so you can achieve the right things.

Stop chasing other people's dreams. Start running your own race.

PART 2
Suffer Less

6

Effortless Discipline: How to Win without White-Knuckling Your Way Through Life

> Only disciplined ones are purely free in life, and the undisciplined are slaves to their moods and passions.
> —*Eliud Kipchoge, "The Greatest Marathoner, Ever,"*
> *according to* The New York Times

When I was a young man with big ambitions but almost equally bad habits, my friend Matt Smith referred me to a simple book that changed my life. I've bought hundreds of copies for friends who have experienced similar benefits.

The book is called *The Art of Living: The Classical Manual on Virtue, Happiness and Effectiveness*. You'll find this quote in it from the Stoic philosopher Epictetus. It was the inspiration I needed to make big changes on the path to becoming the man I wanted to be.

> Now is the time to get serious about living your ideals. How long can you afford to put off who you really want to be? Your nobler self cannot wait any longer. Put your principles into practice—now. Stop the excuses and the procrastination. This is your life! You aren't a child anymore. The sooner you set yourself to your spiritual program, the happier you will be. The longer you wait, the more you'll be vulnerable to mediocrity and feel filled with shame and regret because you know you are capable of better. From this instant on, vow to stop disappointing yourself. Separate yourself from the mob. Decide to be extraordinary and do what you need to do—now.

It's time to stop suffering under the weight of your vices in a prison of temptation. You're better than that, and it's time to become your best self.

It's time to exit your undisciplined doom loops, build systems to protect you, and raise your standards to make the right decisions in your life automatically.

In a world where distraction is the default, systems allow you to take consistent action that builds your discipline, improves your life, and eventually changes your identity so you can raise your standards.

Systems are a set of principles or procedures according to which something is done. The right systems allow almost effortless action to take place regardless of someone's belief in themselves. This automatic action builds confidence, which allows someone to change their identity.

Wikipedia says, "Identity is the set of qualities, beliefs, personality traits, appearance, and/or expressions that characterize a person."

The beliefs and traits must align. So to change your identity, the action must be there.

The following chapters will show you how. We'll begin with how to escape the doom loop of undisciplined behaviors so you can drop the bad habits that hold you back.

This is the first step towards creating freedom through discipline and allows you to start creating higher standards for yourself.

7

Exit the Doom Loop: Ending the Cycle of Failure and Frustration

It's time to be defined by a vision of the future instead of the memories of the past.
—Dr. Joe Dispenza

Back in my college years, I worked in a factory every summer to pay for tuition. Each morning at 9:10 a.m., the company "horn" would sound. Machines shut down, and, like Pavlov's dogs, the workers went outside for a cigarette break. This happened all year round, even in the freezing Canadian winters.

Stimulus = Horn

Response = Have a smoke

Imagine being a worker trying to break that smoking habit. When the horn sounded, the factory worker would immediately reach for his cigarettes. He'd want to go outside to the smoking section and joke with the other workers before heading back inside to boredom, with just enough stimulation running through his veins to make it to lunchtime.

Now, remove the cigarette. And imagine trying to avoid the bad habit. What would the factory worker do? How would they fill the void? He'd hate missing out on the banter with the others, so he'd go outside to the smoking area, and the peer pressure to "just have one drag" would destroy any willpower he had. Soon, he'd be smoking again.

Bad habits are a catch-22. The more you do them, the harder they are to break, and the more they doom you. They are contagious, like a virus, and once inside your nervous system, they are incredibly difficult to root out, extract, and replace.

The old saying is wrong. You don't get something "out of your system" by doing it.

You ingrain bad behavior into your system when you do it.

- Every drink makes a future drink more likely.
- Every XXX website visit guarantees another.
- Every morning that you procrastinate on the work that needs to be done, you strengthen the distracting action you've chosen.

- Every time you skip the opportunity to have a difficult discussion, you strengthen your "avoidance muscle."

"No man is free who is not master of himself," said Epictetus.

When you are a slave to distraction, you suffer. When you master your distractions and become disciplined around what matters to you, then you are free. You suffer less.

How does someone build the systems to exit the vicious cycle of an undisciplined doom loop and enter the virtuous cycle of doing the behaviors that lead to success?

That's the challenge for whatever habit you want to replace and discipline you want to build. If you've always done something, it's hard to break free without a circuit breaker in the system. This requires you to

- drop an old action
- replace the old action with a new positive action
- build an environment and systems to support the new positive action

Dropping the old bad habit creates a vacuum. And, as the old saying goes, Nature abhors a vacuum. Something must fill this space.

Your nervous system is like the electrical wiring in your house. The wiring from the light switch to the light will always be there unless you rip out the wiring.

This can be both good and bad. For example, think of riding a bike. Once you've trained your nervous system how to do it, you never forget. It's always wired inside of you.

The same goes for bad habits. If you always respond to the break horn by grabbing a cigarette or to a stressful day by grabbing a drink or cookies, then that habit will always exist unless you rip out the wiring.

That's an ingrained nervous system loop. You run it on autopilot.

To rip out the wiring, you must circumvent your nervous system and exit the doom loop. And once you rip out the wiring, you must replace the empty void with new wiring, or else, the old wiring— the bad habit—returns.

Without proactively jumping into a new good habit, you reactively slip back into old bad habits. These bad habits then strengthen themselves with each repetition. That's why two days in a row of eating donuts (your old bad habit) is more potent than twenty-one days in a row of eating a veggie omelet (your new good habit).

The strength of the wiring determines your behavior. The longer you go without the bad habit, the weaker the wiring becomes. Weakening the old wiring while strengthening the new is your goal. The best way to do this is with strong systems.

Now, I know you're thinking, "That this sounds too difficult." But it's not. You've already built successful systems in many areas of your life. For example, you might have a working system for household budgeting, going to the gym regularly, getting up on time without hitting snooze, or even walking the dog on the same route every morning. This proves you can build systems, and you can do this for any area of your life.

How long does it take to build the systems to overcome an old bad habit and build a new good one? It varies.

- I quit swearing in four days.
- I quit drinking after four years.
- I have helped friends quit pornography overnight.
- I have helped people become consistent with fitness in just a few weeks.

The Darkside of Discipline

Your mileage will vary, often depending on whether your problem is simply a bad habit or if it qualifies as a legitimate addiction.

While drinking took longer for me to beat, making the decision to elevate my personal standards made the desire for the vice disappear practically overnight.

The most important place for you right now is to put your focus on building the effortless discipline systems.

The results will come—often faster and easier than you might expect.

8

HALT: The Real Reason We Self-Sabotage

> If you're proactive, you focus on preparing.
> If you're reactive, you end up focusing on repairing.
> —*John C. Maxwell*

Why do we come into the house, grab a bag of chips, plop down on the couch, and stress eat while binging Netflix? Why do we snap at the family dog when we've had a long day at work?

Dr. Kevin Downing, a licensed marriage and family therapist, shared an acronym with me—HALT—that explains most of our bad behavior.

The Darkside of Discipline

"We act out when we are Hungry, Angry, Lonely, or Tired," Dr. Downing said.

Think about the last time you had a miserable day at work. You endured endless meetings, took no time to eat, and no one wanted to hear your complaints. Your willpower and discipline had been depleted, like a marathoner's muscle energy stores. You drove home in a daze, walked into the house, and something—*something oh-so-small*—set you off.

Under any other circumstance, the dirty dish on the counter, the coat on the floor, the dog jumping up on your work clothes would not have bothered you much.

But you're hungry (or "hangry," as the Betty White Snickers commercial might say), angry, lonely, and tired. You act out. Whether it's snapping at someone or retreating to booze, Netflix, pornography, or another vice, you take the path of least resistance.

You're in a doom loop, and you need to break out of it—for everyone's sake and the sake of your Big Why.

You need to apply circuit breakers in the forms of preparation, elimination, and accountability.

Most people don't think far enough ahead. They don't plan for a good habit to replace the vice, and consequently, they default back to the old system. Think about what you are trying to change. Are you trying to drop the morning donut or evening alcohol habit? If yes, what will you replace it with, and how will you make it easier—friction-free—to default to the better behavior? How can you make discipline automatic? Getting the donuts and alcohol out of the house, of course, is key. But more preparation and accountability are required, too. You need to prepare something to replace the vice, and you need to be held accountable for your actions.

If you want to halt your suffering, the first step is to identify the HALT triggers and toxic temptations that put you in a doom loop so that you can build systems (using the formula below) to break free.

Your nobler self cannot wait.

How to Stop Watching Porn

It's time to touch on the touchy subject of touching yourself, which most people don't want to touch. This topic touches so many other areas of your life in the wrong way that it cannot be ignored.

The harsh truth is that how we behave in private is reflected in how people see us in public. There's no hiding the shame in our eyes.

Breaking a promise to yourself and the vision of your future—and acting out of alignment with who you want to be—is the fastest way to destroy your self-confidence.

But the vice of watching pornography goes beyond what it does to us personally. We also can't ignore these statistics:

- Seventy percent of men aged 18 to 34 visit a porn site in a typical month.
- Fifteen percent of men are addicted to pornography.
- Thirty-six percent of porn stars were molested as children.
- Ninety percent of children aged 8 to 16 have viewed pornography.

Each statistic is disturbing on its own, but, for me, the worst is the last one.

If you watch pornography, you're to blame for supporting these numbers. Every time you watch porn, you are maintaining an industry of lowlifes and feeding a vicious cycle of anti-social, immoral, and criminal behavior. There is no way to sugarcoat the consumption of pornography. It is not simply a matter of "consenting adults." That's a big lie.

The good news is that quitting porn is simple.

There are two ways to do it. First, using Effortless Discipline Systems. Second, using Standards. The second is faster but requires you to evolve to a higher level of personal integrity. We'll get to that in part 3.

Let's focus first on building systems and designing your environment to destroy the toxic temptations and make the right actions automatic.

Step 1 is to identify your Big Why. Why does this matter to you, and why do you want to stop this suffering? Your Big Why will keep you motivated, and a clear, specific goal provides a direction for creating your systems.

Next, we apply the powerful principle of discipline through subtraction. You must remove toxic temptations. Use a website blocker or app blocker, like the Opal App, so you are no longer able to access XXX content. Remove other temptations and triggers that get you thinking about XXX content (such as following certain people on social media).

Disassociate with any people that promote bad behavior (such as friends who send you porn). Ask them to stop or block them. Every toxic temptation must be eliminated.

Now that we have exited the doom loop, you must fill the void. If viewing XXX content was a routine for you, then you need to put in place a different and positive activity to replace the bad. Set up your environment to make the right actions automatic.

Track your progress and adjust your systems so you continuously improve their effectiveness. If you make a wrong decision, take time to reflect on the trigger that took you off the path to success. Go back to discipline through subtraction and destroy that distraction so you never get off track again.

Add in accountability to someone you deeply do not want to disappoint. This will move mountains in your life. Share your goal with someone that you do not want to let down. Have them hold you accountable via daily check-ins.

You will build confidence when you make a promise and keep that promise, whether it is to yourself or others. This allows you to shift your identity and see yourself as a person who no longer engages in bad behavior or suffers under the weight of vices.

Your nobler self cannot wait.

9

The Doom Loop Escape Plan

> Between stimulus and response, there is a space. In that space is our power to choose our response. In our response lies our growth and freedom.
> —*Viktor Frankl*

Picture in your mind a memory where you acted as your big self; you defied temptation, avoided the path of least resistance, took the high road, and behaved as an evolved individual.

Perhaps this was in a moment of conflict with your spouse or children, in a moment of temptation late at night in the kitchen, or in the face of peer pressure at a restaurant or bar.

Close your eyes and watch yourself with outside eyes at that moment. Feel the moment internally. Sit in this for a minute. Be proud of yourself. This is what you are capable of, and more, always.

Now, switch to a moment where a challenge may have gotten the best of us. We weren't our best selves in a moment of conflict or temptation. I'm thinking about a time when I yelled at my dog for eating garbage she found at the park. It had been a long day after a night of little sleep, and I acted out.

When we let little problems build up, decrease our stress tolerance window, and act out at something small, it doesn't make us a bad person or a failure. We are all human. Just recognize sometimes we are not our best selves. Don't beat yourself up. We're only visiting this quickly to contrast and compare what makes the difference between our big self and our average self. Exhale and forgive yourself.

Examine this action with outside eyes and see where you could have done better in the moment and in preparation for the moment. What led to this performance? Were you hungry, angry, lonely, or tired? Did conflict at work lead to an "off" performance at home? Now that we know the triggers that bring us down, we can begin to build the systems that set us free and stop the suffering.

We must better control our environment going forward. We must set better intentions. We must hold ourselves to higher standards.

This goes for when you walk into your house after a tough day at work, when you get ready to "hop on a Zoom," before you start a team meeting, when you go to the gym, and even when you take the dog for a walk.

To exit your undisciplined doom loop, ask yourself these questions:

1. What's the bad habit to replace?
2. What's the good habit to replace it with?

3. What can make it harder to do the bad?
4. What can make it easier to do the good?

For example, you may want to:

- start exercising consistently
- stop working so much
- quit nighttime weed
- give up swearing
- lose weight
- quit Netflix
- stop watching porn

If you try to exit the loop on willpower alone, you won't succeed.

This is where you run up against a wall. Most strugglers quit here.

Some Wild Horses will try to run through the wall, but that does not work long-term.

The solution is building systems to make the right action automatic. When you make the right decision, you'll get a positive dopamine hit. This strengthens your motivation and provides momentum to come back and keep doing the work tomorrow. Make a promise and keep the promises you make daily.

That's how you escape the *undisciplined doom loop*.

The good news is that you can set up systems to be your Big Self in every situation. You are capable of so much more. That is the power within you. The rest of this book will show you how.

10

Systems: Willpower is Weakness, Structure Equals Freedom

> Efficiency is doing things right; effectiveness is doing the right things. Systems ensure you achieve both.
> —*Peter Drucker*

In Greek mythology, Sisyphus was a devious tyrant who greatly angered the gods. As punishment, the gods forced Sisyphus to roll an immense boulder up a hill, only for it to roll back down every time it neared the top. He was sentenced to repeat this task for eternity.

The Darkside of Discipline

For many people, the pursuit of discipline seems Sisyphean. Inertia stops most people from starting. Discipline is suffering, they say, and so they suffer even more through procrastination rather than bother with any sacrifice. Others make things so challenging, they quickly quit. Lifelong change becomes elusive and demoralizing.

Imagine a different approach. Imagine setting up your self-discipline systems so that instead of rolling a rock up a hill, developing discipline was as easy as rolling the rock downhill.

Let me introduce you to Craiggyphus, the tyrant of Systems who shows you how to become self-disciplined using a plan that gives you momentum without misery.

What many people get wrong about self-discipline is thinking that doing the right things leads to suffering. Actually, it's the reverse.

Doing the right things (getting up early, eating right, doing the work, focusing on what matters) might cause "superficial suffering" in the short term. However, doing the wrong things—procrastinating, binge eating, getting drunk, lying, cheating, being lazy—leads to deep, even eternal suffering: short-term gain but *long*, long-term pain.

Building systems subtracts the suffering that comes with living a life of regrets.

In terms of discipline and habits, we use systems to make the right decisions automatically to perform the right behaviors that achieve the right results.

In our case, specifically, systems set you up to put a Level 10 effort into your Level 10 problem automatically, without overthinking, procrastination, or failure.

Your systems will accelerate your success and automatically knock down positive dominoes in your day, giving you momentum and motivation.

You build systems through the simple process of reverse engineering your goals. We take stock of the current situation.

We identify the obstacles in the way that must be destroyed or removed. We build plans and contingency plans for escaping the doom loop of bad behaviors. Then, we fill that void with good behaviors, and we build systems to make the bad habits harder to do and the good habits easier to do. Over time, the system leads to automation so that your response is as automatic as getting out of bed and going pee first thing in the morning.

It can take as little as a few days for the new system to work almost perfectly.

It's how I quit binge drinking, swearing, overeating, procrastinating, and nearly every bad habit known to man.

Done this way, self-discipline subtracts the suffering, makes success automatic, and delivers effortless discipline for life. The right systems will automatically push you to progress. They are friction-free and help you toss out temptations and destroy distractions. They make success as effortless as rolling a rock downhill.

How to Build Out a System for Effortless Discipline

Building a system isn't just about willpower or discipline—it's about designing an environment and a process that makes success automatic and failure unlikely. Follow these six steps to create systems that work:

1. Start with Clarity: Define Your Goal and Big Why

Begin by identifying the specific goal you want to achieve. Ask yourself:

- What do I want to accomplish?
- Why does this matter to me?

Your Big Why will keep you motivated, and a clear, specific goal provides a direction for your system.

Example:
Goal: Wake up at 5:30 a.m. daily to exercise.
Big Why: To have more energy, improve my health, and be a role model for my family.

2. Reverse Engineer the Outcome: Plan Backward

Visualize the result and work backward to identify the steps needed to achieve it. Think about:

- What actions lead to success?
- What obstacles must be overcome?

Example:
To wake up at 5:30 a.m. to exercise, you need to:

- Go to bed by 10:00 p.m.
- Avoid using your phone after 9:00 p.m.
- Prepare workout clothes the night before.

3. Eliminate Obstacles: Subtract the Suffering

Identify and remove anything that creates friction or makes it harder to take action. Reduce the influence of toxic temptations, distractions, or environments that lead to failure.

Example:

- Move your phone to another room to avoid snoozing your alarm.
- Stop watching TV past 9:00 p.m. to ensure you wind down effectively.

4. Automate Positive Actions: Build Triggers and Cues

Design your environment to make the right actions automatic. Use triggers, cues, and preparation to grease the groove for success.

Example:

- Place your workout clothes next to your bed.
- Set a nightly alarm at 9:00 p.m. as a reminder to start your wind-down routine.

5. Create Accountability: Share Your Commitment

Find a trusted accountability partner or public platform to share your goal and track your progress. Knowing someone else is watching will increase your chances of staying on track.

Example:

- Tell your spouse or coach about your goal and ask them to check in daily.
- Use an app or a physical checklist to track progress.

6. Test, Track, and Adjust: Improve Continuously

Reflect on your results regularly. What's working? What's not? Use these insights to refine your system until it becomes effortless and sustainable.

Example:
If you're still hitting snooze, experiment with an earlier bedtime or use a louder alarm. Reflect weekly on your progress and fine-tune the system.

Summary of the System-Building Process:

1. **Clarity:** Define your goal and Big Why.
2. **Reverse Engineer:** Plan the steps needed to achieve your goal.
3. **Eliminate Obstacles:** Remove distractions and temptations.
4. **Automate Actions:** Use triggers and cues to make the right behavior automatic.
5. **Create Accountability:** Share your commitment with people you trust and deeply don't want to disappoint.
6. **Test and Adjust:** Reflect and refine until your system becomes second nature.

With these steps, you'll build a system that removes resistance, supports consistent action, and helps you achieve effortless discipline.

How I Quit Drinking

I grew up in a small city in Canada. Teenagers in my town played hockey and drank beer or drank beer and played hockey. The order didn't matter. I started binge drinking at the age of sixteen.

I remained a frat-boy-style binge-drinker on and off for the next fifteen years. It led to stupid decisions, a couple of fistfights, and three episodes of drinking and driving. I survived all of them and stayed out of jail only by the Grace of God.

My binge drinking continued until I was a thirty-year-old hypocritical personal trainer. From Monday to Friday, I was the model of discipline. I rose early and was in the gym from 6:00 a.m. to 6:00 p.m., training Canada's wealthiest people and doing my own workouts that led to six-pack abs and three-hundred-pound bench presses. At the same time, I was writing for *Men's Health* magazine and growing my own online fitness brand, Turbulence Training.

On weekends, though, I did a reverse Clark Kent, transforming from superhero to drunken zero. Drinking began in the early afternoon on Saturday and continued to early Sunday morning. Sundays meant hangovers, regrets, and anxiety.

On January 1, 2006, I experienced the lowest moment of my life. I cover the details in my book *Unstoppable*. After a long, lonely day, thinking I was going to have a heart attack and die in my apartment, I ended up in the emergency room at 11:00 p.m., suffering from an anxiety attack.

After a few hours, the kind doctors and nurses sent me home, and I cleaned myself up for six weeks. Then, I fell back into old bad habits and found myself binging again on weekends.

The next episode happened in late March. This time, I let the anxiety attack go on for six weeks, twenty-four hours a day until I finally gave in and went to the ER again. It was one of the most embarrassing moments of my life.

Shame is a powerful force. I decided to let go of my old ways.

But the funny thing was that everything else in my life was almost perfect. I was making more money than ever. I had many wonderful friends. I was in the best shape of my life. I just needed to clean up the rest.

The first thing I did was remove myself from the toxic environments. If you want to guarantee you'll fall back into a bad habit of drinking, go to a bar. So, I didn't. I spent less time with friends who wanted me to go out drinking. I made new friends and found healthier places to spend my time.

Things went well, but not perfectly. I relapsed a few times and paid the price. But each time I did wrong, there was one thing I did right—self-reflection. I reviewed the movie of my life and looked for the place where I went wrong.

For the next few years, I muddled in the world of "social drinkers." I'd have one to two drinks one to two times per month, except for when I didn't. Once or twice per year, I'd go off the rails with three, four, or even six drinks. The pain of regret was always greater than the pain of the hangover.

It wasn't until meeting my wife and watching her give up alcohol completely that I finally put in place the missing system—accountability to someone I deeply did not want to disappoint. Following her lead, I gave up booze forever in November 2021.

Looking back, it was easy to change what I did. It was also easy to change who I did things with. Today, I can't believe I wasted all those days and nights on alcohol.

11

Elimination: Subtract the Suffering and Cut the Chaos

> Change is a matter of choice, not calendar. You can just as easily change your life today as on New Year's Day.
> —*Dan S. Kennedy*

Imagine you and I are about to run the Boston Marathon. Before the race starts, an official walks over. He offers you the world's best running shoes. These are the same shoes used by the world's top marathoners to shave thirty seconds from their race time. He hands a backpack to me. It's filled with thirty pounds of sand. I'm told to wear it for the duration of the race.

The Darkside of Discipline

Which of these will have a greater impact on our performance? The backpack, of course.

Now, imagine I remove the backpack—my performance will dramatically improve. Adding the "world's best shoes" (or, in our case, another good habit) might make a small difference. But removing a negative will make a huge difference.

It's a blunt analogy for life and discipline. Most people go through life desperately seeking another minor hack (like cold plunges) that only improves their performance by 0.01 percent while carrying a millstone of mistakes on their backs.

However, the easiest way to achieve more discipline is by eliminating toxic temptations and destructive distractions. Discipline is a matter of subtraction, not addition.

- What good is a green juice when you drink a bottle of wine each night?
- What good is reading ten pages a day when you spend two hours mindlessly scrolling on social media?
- What good is telling your wife you love her when you watch porn without her knowing?

It's always the bad habits in life that pull us down far more than good habits can lift us up. If you remove the weights from your life, your performance will skyrocket.

The fastest way to achieve more is by saying *no* more often. These are the two most important letters to instill discipline.

As Dr. Peter Attia explains in his book *Outlive*, saying "yes" too often and overcommitting decreases your capacity for emotional regulation. This leads to increased stress, outbursts, and moments of "acting out" (anger, emotional binge-eating, drinking to get drunk, or even retreating to a Netflix binge session to numb yourself).

When this happens, you procrastinate, hold back, get nothing done, and get nowhere on what matters.

Elimination: Subtract the Suffering and Cut the Chaos

When you say "yes" to something that doesn't matter, you say "NO!" to your goals and dreams.

But when you're "selfish" and say "NO!" to the minor things, you can major in the major things and say "YES" to achieve more this year than ever before. Being "selfish" is one of the most generous things you can do because it allows you to get more done on what matters and help more people more significantly. But if you say "yes" to every little request, your productivity, goals, and dreams "die a death of one thousand cuts."

*If you want to do great things,
you have to do fewer things.*

Please read that again. And maybe again. Print it out. Put it beside your computer.

At the very least, promise me that instead of saying "yes" to every request, you will at least use Meatloaf's approach, telling the asking party, "Let me sleep on it, and I'll give you an answer in the morning." (Sing it now.)

If you want to do great things, you have to do fewer things.

One of the secrets to success is to be more disciplined in where you say yes and when you say no. With this practice in place, it reduces the risk of getting so overwhelmed that you act out.

The same principle applies to having "discipline" around your diet.

Years ago, I went to Tuscany, Italy, with a travel group of entrepreneurs. For ten days, we explored the wine region, drove Ferraris (at painfully slow speeds) on the roads between Florence and Sienna, and ate decadent meals.

Our group was a near split of overweight and lean individuals. One habit stood out. Between meals, the lean individuals engaged in some type of activity, while the overweight individuals snacked, drank more wine, and consumed more calories.

Despite eating four-course meals twice per day (plus a buffet breakfast), the lean individuals gained no weight (or lost weight, in some cases), while the overweight group gained several pounds.

This is by no means a scientific study; however, it supports the principles of building parameters to say NO.

As a health and nutrition expert for over twenty-five years, I've helped tens of thousands of people on their weight-loss journeys. And no matter what the latest diet guru is trying to peddle, weight loss (and fat loss) comes down to calories in, calories out.

No eating between meals, no eating after 8:00 p.m., and no liquid calories. If you followed those three simple lines on a checklist, you'd increase your ability to lose weight.

It's a system for saying NO that delivers almost automatic results.

By the same logic, apply the parameters checklist to your *not* to-do list.

Staying out of trouble is far more important than adding tiny life hacks. And saying *no* to too many projects is essential to protect your emotional regulation buffer zone so that the stress doesn't skyrocket, leading to an outburst that puts you off track.

When you choose success through subtraction, you make the path smoother by eliminating the obstacles in your way.

Elimination: Subtract the Suffering and Cut the Chaos

Sometimes, we need help and hacks to say *no*. "Being busy is not a badge of honor," says Daniel Woodrum, my co-author and our head business coach at Early to Rise.

Daniel knows that next-level discipline and achieving higher standards is about accomplishing more with less activity. It's about being proactive, not reactive.

One of Daniel's secret weapons in his pursuit of discipline is the Opal App. Like most of us, Daniel's phone is the source of temptation and distraction. As an entrepreneur and coach of other high-performing business owners, Daniel's to-do list feels never-ending, and he receives messages 24/7.

One night, on the couch at home, Daniel had a moment that hit him in the heart. He was supposed to be talking to his daughter, but the temptation of the phone beside him distracted his attention. Soon, he was replying to a message.

"Daddy, put your phone away," his daughter said.

That was his "enough" moment. He knew he had to start saying *no* to his phone so he could say *yes* to his family. Soon after, Daniel discovered the Opal app.

Every day from 5:00 to 8:00 a.m. Daniel uses the Opal app on his phone so it blocks his ability to access apps, email, and text messages. This is Daniel's most important work block of the day. He destroys distractions and dominates his to-do list.

At night, from 5:00 to 8:00 p.m., Daniel activates the Opal app again. This time, it supports his ability to be present with his family at home. He and his wife have three kids under six years old, and the Opal app helps him be present at dinner, bath time, bedtime, and quality time with his wife.

It was a simple solution that provided the subtraction Daniel needed to develop effortless discipline. His life is so much better because of what he removed, not what he added.

Exercise: Make a *Not* to-do list

The 80-20 principle states that 80 percent of your problems come from 20 percent of your mistakes.

Now is the time for you to make a *not* to-do list that destroys distractions, tosses your toxic temptations, and negates the negative people and environments from your life.

For example, if you procrastinate in the morning, it is most likely due to the fact that you wake up, open your phone, and get sucked into addictive apps designed to steal your attention. You need to build a fence around yourself.

In this case, a *not* to-do list would look like this:

- I do *not* take my phone out of airplane mode for 90 minutes after I wake up.
- I do *not* check social media until after lunch.
- I do *not* keep my phone in my bedroom.

Over to you. Pick your poison and build a *not* to-do list that keeps you safe from harm.

12

Preparation: Grease the Groove and Automate Your Wins

> More important than the will to win is the will to prepare.
> —*Charlie Munger*

When you first hear the name, Axl Rose, your mind doesn't immediately jump to planning and preparation—more like mayhem and destruction. But Axl was a preparation fanatic.

The Darkside of Discipline

"I do warm-ups religiously," he said in a radio interview. "It's not manly to do voice exercises, but you gotta do what you gotta do."

According to this YouTube video (http://bit.ly/42F14Av), touring with Axl in the 1990s involved a painstaking four to five-hour routine of exercise, massage, and chiropractic. The chiropractor even stood at the side of the stage during the Use Your Illusion tour to adjust Axl between songs. He also had an on-stage health consultant apply a humidifier to his throat and deliver him various teas as the concert went on.

As a father of three children under the age of three, a much less glamorous life phase than being a rock'n'roll star, I've discovered that planning and preparation is the key to good parenting.

Keeping a constant supply of diapers, ensuring the diaper bag isn't missing a critical onesie for an emergency "blowout" change, and finding the right nighttime routine that helps your kids sleep as much as possible prove that much of good parenting comes down to planning and preparation.

As a productivity guru, I've long taught that planning and preparation are the keys to getting things done. You make your to-do list the day before (not the morning of, that's too late!), you plan your week in advance with my Perfect Week Formula, and you set yourself up in the morning by removing distractions and "eating that frog" (to quote Mark Twain).

If you want to be disciplined, it's no different. Planning and preparation to stay on track with your goals is essential. It's essential to have a *not* to-do list, but you must plan and prepare to follow through on it.

In addition to eliminating procrastination distractions in the morning, you must plan and prepare the night before so you know what to do first instead of checking your phone.

Preparation: Grease the Groove and Automate Your Wins

If you want to achieve anything and make successful behaviors automatic, you need to do better planning and preparation than ever before.

The reason anyone fails to be disciplined or complete any type of transformation is that they have not done enough preparation. Then, when they are put in a tough spot, they make old (bad) choices that are already ingrained in their nervous system. They enter a doom loop that is difficult to escape.

You don't rise to the level of your willpower; you fall to the level of your preparation.

> **You don't rise to the level of your willpower; you fall to the level of your preparation.**

One of the most effective ways to roll the rock downhill is to start with better planning. What looks like hardcore discipline is often just superior preparation.

If you want in-depth advice for planning your days and being more productive, please read my book, *The Perfect Week Formula*. It's available at FreePerfectWeekFormula.com or by scanning this QR code.

How to Stop Hitting Snooze

"I just bought a Sonic Boom Alarm," wrote my client AJ in his weekly email accountability update.

The Amazon description reads: *Turbo charged loud, vibrating alarm clock with adjustable volume and tone. Shakes you awake with a powerful bed shaker and adjustable extra loud alarm.*

"How does your wife like this?" I asked.

"Uh, not so much."

In my twenty-five years as a high-performance coach, once I help people overcome serious vices like booze and porn, "hitting snooze" ranks pretty high on the list of bad habits that hold ambitious people back.

Hitting the snooze button hurts you in three ways. First, you are breaking a promise you made to yourself the night before. This destroys your confidence. Second, you are "telling your hopes and dreams that they can wait," as my friend Bedros Keuilian says. This further erodes belief in yourself. Third, getting back into a light sleep cycle for another ten minutes actually leaves you more tired. By hitting the snooze button, you've knocked down three negative dominoes and set up your day for failure. You'll be rushing around, over-caffeinating, decreasing your stress tolerance window, snapping at your family, and ingraining yourself into a deeper doom loop.

The solution is not a louder alarm. (That should come with a divorce warning.)

You'll find the answer in what you do the night before. The longer I coach, the more I see "getting to bed on time" as an essential component of success. Unfortunately, this advice, as golden as it is, doesn't make for as sexy of social media content compared to plunging into an ice bath or frozen-over lake.

If you want to get up on time, you must get to bed on time. If you want to get to bed on time, you must eliminate the destructive distractions and toss the toxic temptations. In our program, we use a "Reverse Alarm." It's actually the most important alarm you should have on your phone.

When the Reverse Alarm rings, turn off your distractions—the TV, your laptop, your phone. Eliminating electronics is a key to getting to bed on time, falling asleep fast, and sleeping well. When you do this every night, soon you won't need an alarm in the morning. You'll be getting up and feeling refreshed before it goes off.

Add in accountability to someone you deeply do not want to disappoint, and you'll never sleep late again.

13

Accountability: Harness the Power of Positive People

It's easy to be great when you're surrounded by great people.
—*Craig Ballantyne*

There are many clichés in the personal development world that are not true, such as

- You are enough.
- The Universe has your back.
- You are exactly where you need to be.

At best, these are general and impossible-to-prove statements. At worst, these lies operate as excuses for people to avoid doing the work and staying stuck.

But one personal development cliché that is as true as the sun is bright goes like this:

You are the average of the five people you spend the most time with.
—Jim Rohn

Harvard research has found that if one spouse became obese, the likelihood that the other spouse would become obese increased by 37 percent.

Research also shows that smokers who hang out with other smokers have the hardest time quitting smoking (like those people I worked with in the factory decades ago).

Research even shows that if your adolescent child's friend has an authoritative mother (meaning strict), then your child has a 40 percent lower chance of getting drunk. So, choose your child's friend's parents wisely!

What does this mean for you and your habits? It's obvious, isn't it? If your closest social circle drinks alcohol, is overweight, smokes cigarettes or weed, and binge-watches Netflix, you're seeing your future.

How Good People Helped Me Quit a Bad Habit (Drinking)

When I quit drinking, I did two things.

1. I continued my good friendships (with drinkers) in non-drinking environments (hikes, sports, the gym, etc.). I don't believe you have to cut ties with all people from your past like some cold-hearted social media gurus say; however, you must set yourself up for success in social settings.

2. More importantly, I befriended successful, positive people who did not drink alcohol.

In 2009, I met Lewis Howes, *New York Times* bestselling author and host of the top podcast, *The School of Greatness*, through a mutual friend, Carrie Wilkerson.

"I've never had a drop of alcohol," Lewis said.

That statement blew my (binge-drinking) mind and opened it to what was possible.

Today, no one important in my life drinks alcohol. Not my wife nor my personal Tribe of Mentors, successful entrepreneurs such as Bedros Keuilian, Joel Marion, Jason Capital, and Sharran Srivatsaa. Not a single alcoholic drink would be ordered if I took them all to dinner.

Being surrounded by non-drinkers makes my no-drinking decision easy, and it validates that I'm on the right road.

It is also easy to avoid alcohol when I share these stories in books, podcasts, and on my YouTube channel. This is the power of Public Accountability. I've made a promise to you and millions of other readers, and as a man of integrity, it's easy to keep this promise. This, in turn, builds my confidence, strengthens my identity, and makes it possible to achieve the high standards I've set for myself.

But when you keep your goals to yourself, it's easier to break the promises you've made to yourself. A lack of accountability is one of the fastest ways to break your promises, destroy your confidence, and live an undisciplined life.

To be fair, accountability is one of the reasons why online challenges "work" so well. We can argue about the value of the activities, but we can't deny the power of accountability. It is one of the most effective parts of the effortless discipline systems.

Public accountability is one of my secret systems for success. It's what has kept me at 9 percent body fat with six-pack

Accountability: Harness the Power of Positive People

abs (even though they are not necessary!) for the past thirty years.

Public accountability is what helped me beat social anxiety and do the self-development work to meet my wife and get her to fall in love with me.

There are two ways to harness the power of accountability. First, as I've shared in my previous book, *Unstoppable*, "You must have accountability to someone you deeply do not want to disappoint. This is what will help you move mountains in your life." Second, there is the concept of Public Accountability, that is, telling the world, including strangers online, what you're setting out to achieve.

Public Accountability is what I call the "burn the boats" strategy of habit change. Millions of people know that I don't swear and now know I don't drink. In 2011, I started off by telling my email list of 151,000 people that I quit swearing. I've continued sharing that in my books, podcasts, YouTube videos, and on stage at events. Everyone knows it.

That first email was a "burn the boats" moment. Once you've told the world, there is no going back.

The only downside is that this technique is so simple and so powerful—for people with integrity—that you'll be tempted to dismiss it.

Commit to this principle: "Do what you say you'll do." You can move mountains in your life when you tell the world who you are and how you act.

How I Quit Swearing in Four Days

I was sprinting up a hill through the woods one morning when it hit me.

"You never swear in front of your mother, and you never swear on stage, so why do you swear like a sailor when you're around your friends?"

I wanted to be a good, honorable family man, the type of father figure found on old black-and-white TV shows and the kind of man that my father struggled to be.

My dad was not a role model for my goals. I guarantee he invented new combinations of swear words when we were fixing his tractors on freezing mornings on the farm where I grew up. Meanwhile, my mom made sure I went to church every Sunday and kept me out of trouble.

By this point in my career, I had become "internet-famous" in the fitness industry with hundreds of thousands of followers. I never swore in my YouTube videos, when I spoke at fitness or business seminars, or in front of my family.

"You tell people how to change their lives every day in your emails," I said to myself, "Why don't you change yours?"

And with that, I decided to quit swearing.

So, I took action. After aligning my actions with my Big Why, the next thing I did was to email my audience and tell them, "I quit swearing." Remember that public accountability—provided you have integrity—can get you to change your behavior virtually overnight.

It's so simple you'll want to reject this idea. But my results prove it works.

I swore six times the first day, four times the second day, and then twice per day for two more days. Then it was done. No more swearing.

If you want to move mountains in your life, telling the world works wonders.

What If You Don't Have a Circle of People?

I know what you're thinking, "But I don't have positive people in my life."

Not having your tribe is holding you back.

Negative people and negative environments are the biggest destroyers of dreams. You can't let the contagious disease of disappointment into your life.

If you live on a lonely entrepreneur island surrounded by people with no ambition, where no one sets goals, and no one has personal discipline, then you're setting yourself up to fail.

This is why it's so darn important to find your tribe.

You must get connected with a peer group of like-minded, ambitious men and women with big goals and dreams.

A rising tide can lift all boats, but the heavy anchor of bad habits will weigh you down and drown you. If you want to change your life, *nothing* is more important than choosing who you spend your time with.

The more good people you know, the easier everything in your life will be.

EXERCISE: Find Your Tribe

It's time to find people that will help you go to the next level in life.

First, identify what you wish to change and whom you aspire to be like.

Second, recognize where these types of people tend to congregate and do your best to get in those rooms. An added plus: spending time "online" with good people works well too.

You can find these people at business conferences, industry events, church, the gym, and through asking successful people where they go to connect with other successful people.

We have even created an online community of like-minded, positive people for you to join—for free—called The Millionaire Mentorship. Please visit DarkSideofDiscipline.com/tribe or scan this QR code for access.

If you're a business owner that wants to get off "lonely entrepreneur island" and connect with other like minded business owners, I run three live events every year that would be perfect for you. Please email me at Craig@CraigBallantyne.com for more information.

The Power of 3

I'm going to let you in on the *secret* of our top coaching clients...

Daniel and I work with hundreds of entrepreneurs who have turned their lives and businesses around because of this one simple technique.

It's called The Power of 3 and is a daily accountability tactic.

It's a simple set of questions that keep you on track to your definition of success.

You must choose three simple but important questions to answer at the end of each day. For example:

1. Did I wake up at 6:00 a.m.? If not, why not?
2. Did I spend sixty minutes on my most important task before checking my email? If not, why not?
3. Did I avoid alcohol? If not, why not?

The power is in answering the second part of each question: If not, why not?

This gives you powerful self-reflection and introspection to identify your Level 10 problems in life, moving you into a position to put in a corresponding Level 10 effort.

Answering these three questions daily keeps you on track and allows your coach or accountability partner to help you fix your mistakes.

If you do this for twenty-one days, or preferably sixty days, in a row, you'll cement new good habits and improve your performance. Once you've mastered a habit, remove the related question and replace it with a new question that allows you to level up again.

Repeat the Power of 3 over and over, and you'll achieve your big goals and dreams faster.

14

Creating Effortless Discipline Systems: Making the Right Decisions Automatic

Habits are friction-based. No matter whether good or bad, if an action is friction-free, and the groove has been greased, then you will choose this habit because it is the path of least resistance.

You must make the bad habit as difficult as possible and the good habit is easy as possible.

You must put more friction in front of the bad habit. You must grease the groove of the good habit through better planning and preparation. You must eliminate all environmental

Creating Effortless Discipline Systems: Making the Right Decisions Automatic

friction to make the right choice. This includes the people you surround yourself with on this journey.

For example, want to cut your daily phone screen time from four hours to ninety minutes? If you wake up in the morning and start scrolling and keep your phone beside you all day while you're working (and driving!), you've made it too easy to continue the bad behavior. You need to add friction, such as storing your phone in another room, keeping it in airplane mode, using the Opal app, and even turning it off. You also need to grease the groove for better behaviors, such as setting alarms twice a day to go for walks outside (that serve as better break replacements to scrolling social media). Add another layer of grease by joining a group of like-minded, positive people who share the same goals as you, and check in with them every day.

Break the cycle.

Support the change.

Make the right actions automatic.

Everything comes down to taking the first step.

"Pushing yourself to take simple actions creates a chain reaction in your confidence and your productivity," says Mel Robbins, author of *The 5 Second Rule: Transform Your Life, Work, and Confidence with Everyday Courage.*

The first step gives you momentum and motivation and gets you going. Without the first step, you'll never fix a problem. Keep this list close at hand while you develop your standards.

1. Identify the bad habit to change.
2. Identify a good new habit to replace the bad.
3. Make it as hard as possible, using systems to repeat the bad habit (subtraction).
4. Make it as easy as possible, using systems, to complete the good new habit.

5. Reflect on your results, plan and prepare better, and improve the systems daily.
6. Get accountability from someone you deeply do not want to disappoint so that you stick to this plan.
7. Refer back to your big why and specific definition of success to stay on track. When your reason why is great enough and your intention clear enough, you will learn to be consistent.
8. Change your identity and story around who you are when it comes to the old bad habit.
9. Set higher standards for yourself and stick to them.

If you are consistent, then you'll be persistent. If you're persistent, you'll win.

How to Get Back on Track

No one quits smoking on their first try. Even I fall back on bad behaviors from time to time when my willpower runs out.

"We don't rise to the level of our expectations," the Greek poet and soldier Archilochus said, "We fall to the levels of our training."

James Clear said it better:

"You do not rise to the level of your goals. You fall to the level of your systems."

Years ago, when I had the bad habit of binge-eating chocolate-covered almonds, it took me a year to figure out the system for success. First, I had to notice that it only happened after having three drinks, which lowered my inhibitions. Then, I had to cut back from three drinks to two to see if it still happened. It did, but less frequently. Next, I built systems to have only half a drink and incorporated public accountability.

Creating Effortless Discipline Systems: Making the Right Decisions Automatic

But on those mornings when I had failed the night before, and I woke up sweating, with a full stomach and milk chocolate running through my veins, I knew I had to develop a mantra to give myself grace and get back on track.

"Every minute I'm awake is a minute I move away from my mistake," I told myself.

I'd finish my morning work block with a full belly but feeling a little better. My morning walk helped with digestion, and I started to feel like myself again. Another work block, then a workout, and a healthy lunch, and I was back to normal.

"Win or learn," I told myself, and learn I did.

Life is never a one-time win-or-lose situation. You have time to turn your life, habits, and discipline around on any day.

So, if you've fallen off track, do one thing right now to get back on plan. Review and rebuild your systems.

- Build a fence around yourself and toss the toxic temptations.
- Rewire your routines so they are automatic and more effective.
- Keep the junk out of your life—the junk food, the junk relationships, the junk thoughts, the junk habits.
- And lean on your social support and public accountability—the power of positive people—to get back on track, stay on track, build your confidence one action at a time, and change your identity for life.

To get back on track, remember that one missed day doesn't destroy everything unless you let it. You have the tools to break the vicious cycle and get back on track.

PART 3
Achieve More

15

The Fastest Path to Freedom and Success

> Never Peak. The best is yet to come.
> —*Bedros Keuilian*

Congratulations! You've reached a pivotal moment in your journey—a moment where systems, habits, and discipline have laid a strong foundation for success. But to achieve more and never peak, it's not enough to rely solely on systems. True transformation requires something deeper: aligning your identity with your standards.

Standards are the invisible rules that shape the way we live, work, and interact with the world. They define what we tolerate, what we pursue, and how we show up daily. Without clear, non-negotiable standards, even the best systems can falter under the weight of inconsistency. But when standards are rooted in your identity, they become the unshakable framework for peak performance. Standards aren't just what you do—they're who you are.

To elevate your standards and achieve more, you must first evolve your identity. Who you believe yourself to be directly influences the habits you form, the actions you take, and the results you achieve. Your identity is the lens through which you see every opportunity and challenge, and by aligning it with your standards, you set the stage for lasting success.

Understanding and evolving your identity is the first step to bridging the gap between who you are today and who you have the potential to become.

How to Stop Watching Porn, Part 2

Earlier, we gave you a list of actions to build effortless discipline systems that eliminate the temptation to look at pornography.

To be honest, it takes work, planning, preparation, and time to ingrain these systems into your nervous system and replace the doom loop of undisciplined desires.

What if there was an easier, faster way to kick pornography to the curb?

There is: through standards.

No online challenges are needed, and there is no reason to spend hundreds of dollars on a course that promises to cure you of your addiction.

You simply become the type of person that does not look at porn.

Earlier in the book, you created your Big Why. If you're a man, chances are it is centered around being successful, having a happy marriage, and raising happy, healthy, well-adjusted children.

Pornography is in complete and utter misalignment with each value of your Big Why.

That's why it causes you so much stress, guilt, and anxiety when you consume it.

You don't need discipline hacks or systems to avoid it. You simply step up and announce to yourself, "I am not a man that watches porn."

Now, you might be thinking, "That won't work."

But if you're a man with a strong identity anchored in alignment with his Big Why, it will. If you need to get there, then go back to building the systems, making and keeping promises to yourself, building your confidence, and shifting your identity.

16

Identity: Who You are is What You Do

Your beliefs become your thoughts,
Your thoughts become your words,
Your words become your actions,
Your actions become your habits,
Your habits become your values,
Your values become your destiny.
—*Gandhi*

In 2007, Justin Kan had an idea: what if he wore a camera 24/7, documenting his life? The concept isn't about the content; it's about integrity. Imagine if a camera recorded your every move. Would it change how you act? Would you still hit the snooze button, watch one more show on Netflix after your bedtime, or have 'just one more small glass of wine"?

Integrity is who you are when no one is watching. For me, living as if the camera is always on has become a cornerstone of my identity. It's far more impactful than chasing trends or completing random challenges. Integrity is foundational, eternal, and far more powerful than any to-do list.

What about your integrity? Do you know who you need to be? More importantly, are you living it?

For instance, my identity is rooted in my personal integrity. My values and vision drive every decision.

Your identity is the foundation upon which your habits, actions, and, ultimately, your destiny are built. Gandhi's quote highlights how your beliefs and thoughts are the seeds that grow into the visible outcomes of your life. This means that every action, no matter how small, reflects and reinforces the person you are becoming.

To build an identity that aligns with your values and vision, you must actively engage in self-reflection. It's not enough to rely on wishful thinking or fleeting motivation. You need to take stock of your habits, decisions, and the standards you're living by.

As my friend and leadership expert Jon Gordon said in his book *You Win in the Locker Room First*, "As a leader, it is so important that you words equal your actions. It is imperative that you make sure that you go through a self-evaluation process on an almost daily basis to make sure that your actions are in line with your words. You must do what you say and say what you do."

Are your actions guiding you toward the person you want to be? Or are they keeping you in a cycle of frustration, resentment, and stagnation? This is where the process of knowing yourself becomes critical. By auditing your daily actions and habits, you create the clarity needed to close the gap between who you are now and who you have the potential to become.

Phil Heath, one of the greatest bodybuilders of all time, embodied this principle. His story demonstrates how understanding and auditing your performance can transform your mindset and elevate your standards, setting the stage for extraordinary success.

Know Yourself: Watching the Game Tape

Phil Heath won the Mr. Olympia title (the "World Series" of bodybuilding) seven times in a row. But his biggest lesson didn't come from his wins; it came from the failure he suffered the year before his first victory.

"If you want to win in life," he said, "You have to audit your performance. You have to watch the game tape."

"When I came in second in the 2010 Olympia, and my rival Jay Cutler's name was called as the winner," Phil said, "You could see me exhale with *relief*. I was *not* mentally ready to be a winner."

"But I only realized that after watching the tape and auditing my performance. Doing that inspired me to improve my mental game. And that allowed me to win the next seven years in a row."

I was only able to quit drinking, stop swearing, shed my introverted tendencies, and improve my performance in every area of life after committing to daily self-reflection and introspection.

I teach a simple self-auditing process called "Watching the Movie of Your Day." This practice ties directly into shaping your identity and maintaining high standards. Every day, either late afternoon or early evening, take five minutes to replay the movie of your day, mentally or in a journal. Compare your actions to the script you wrote the day before—your

Identity: Who You are is What You Do

schedule or to-do list. Did your day align with the identity and standards you aim to uphold?

For instance, you might have planned to wake up at 6:00 a.m., work on an important project for thirty minutes, exercise before the kids get up, finish work by 5:00 p.m., and eat a healthy meal with your family at the dinner table without your phone. This ideal day reflects the standards of someone disciplined and committed to their priorities.

However, if you hit snooze, did only fifteen minutes of work on your project, skipped your workout, got home late from work, and ate leftovers alone for dinner while simultaneously scrolling on your phone while talking to your spouse before binge-watching Netflix with a drink, you have a problem.

These deviations likely stem from a lack of alignment with your identity and standards. Perhaps the cycle began the night before when you stayed up late scrolling social media, which disrupted your sleep and caused you to hit the snooze button on your alarm in the morning. Knocking down this first negative domino led to many others—conflict with your spouse, rushing through your work, unhealthy choices, and stress from another chaotic day.

> **Deviations stem from a lack of alignment with your identity and standards.**

This vicious cycle highlights the importance of reflection. By reviewing your day, you can identify the cause-and-effect relationship between poor habits and the resulting lack of discipline the next day.

You'll realize the need for a new standard:

- not drinking alcohol on work nights
- turning off your phone at 9:00 p.m.
- being in bed by 10:00 p.m. every night—no exceptions
- no Netflix

This commitment to higher standards is needed to break free from the chain of negative dominos so you can get on the path to peak performance.

Joining a discipline challenge won't fix the root of these issues. Often, adding more tasks only increases stress and the demands on your time. Instead of chasing someone else's definition of discipline, your Big Why, identity, and standards must guide the changes. By watching the game tape and recognizing your susceptibility to late-night binge-watching, you can seek accountability for this specific change. You can sit down with your spouse to explain why prioritizing sleep is essential for achieving your goals. You can also ask your coach to change the password on your Netflix account until you've built a fourteen-day streak of waking up and going to bed on time.

Within days, the effects of living in alignment with your standards become clear. You wake up on time, energized and excited. You finish work by 5:00 p.m. and take your spouse on a date to reconnect. You spend phone-free time with your kids. These positive outcomes compound, strengthening your identity and raising your standards exponentially, not incrementally, reinforcing your new identity and showing the power of intentional reflection.

Custom Solutions for Personal Growth and Peak Performance

The key to lasting change is creating standards and systems that align with your unique identity and personal goals, not blindly following generic challenges. Reflection allows you to identify the "first cause" of your stress, anxiety, or overwhelm. You can pinpoint problematic habits and address them before they spiral out of control. With small, intentional tweaks, you build discipline and take steps in the right direction.

This process fuels not only better performance but also a stronger sense of self. As John Maxwell writes in *The 21 Irrefutable Laws of Leadership*, "Who you are is who you attract." If you want to surround yourself with successful, growth-minded people, you must first embody those qualities yourself. Your standards reflect your identity, and your identity attracts the environment and relationships that will elevate your life.

Identity Shift: A Foundation for Change

I have a friend named Fun Bobby. Bobby was the ultimate party host and one of the most generous men I know. Almost every weekend, he invited dozens of people to his house to celebrate birthdays and holidays. But Bobby wasn't just known for his hospitality—he was also a heavy drinker. Two or three bottles of wine or Champagne in a single night wasn't unusual for him.

Then, one day, Bobby made a decision that shocked everyone: "I'm not a drinker anymore," he declared. And just like that, he stopped drinking simply from changing his belief about who he was.

What took me fourteen years to accomplish—quitting drinking—Bobby achieved overnight because he embraced an identity shift. This is the power of aligning your actions with your standards and adopting a new identity.

Not everyone quits drinking, swearing, or porn overnight, although it's possible. For most of us, the journey is longer, filled with hundreds, even thousands of small steps. But each step is important.

In *Atomic Habits*, James Clear captures this perfectly: "Every action you take is a vote for the type of person you wish to become." As the votes build up, so does the evidence of your new identity. This is why meaningful change doesn't necessarily require radical transformations. Small, intentional habits provide the evidence needed to shift your identity and raise your standards.

Everything you've learned so far—building a Big Why, creating a specific definition of success, saying no to distractions, tossing toxic temptations, and creating friction-free paths for automatic actions—is a toolkit for helping you build integrity in your actions to support your identity shift.

However, just as there is a dark side to discipline, we need to give you a word of warning about identity.

The Dark Side of Identity

> It's hard to save poor early decisions with good late decisions.
> —*James Clear*

In Peter Thiel's book *Zero to One*, he criticizes the traditional education system:

> Students who don't learn best by sitting still at a desk are made to somehow feel inferior, while children who excel on conventional measures like tests and assignments end up defining their identities in terms of this weirdly contrived academic parallel reality.

As someone who excelled in school due to my good memory, I know how this feels. For many years, I mistakenly thought I was smarter than most people, especially those who didn't go far in school. It's embarrassing to write this, as it sounds so ridiculous. Only after being humbled many times in life can I see that I had created a false identity. In contrast, students who weren't cut out for school were made to feel like failures. These students also suffered from cases of false identity.

Discipline challenges are not different. If you succeed, it doesn't mean you'll be disciplined in other areas of life. Discipline is not automatically transferable. You do not become invincible to temptation and distraction simply because you do a cold plunge every morning. Likewise, if you don't finish the discipline challenge, it can create the wrong identity. You're not a failure because you didn't achieve someone else's definition of discipline. You cannot put your identity into the hands of others.

This is the dark side of building identity. If you get it wrong at the start, with the wrong goal, wrong blueprint, and wrong action steps, you risk becoming the wrong person, wasting time and energy that could have gone into working on your Level 10 problem.

If you choose the wrong identity, you will be misaligned with your values and vision. You will create more stress the more you strengthen this incorrect identity. The further you go off course from that initial direction you chose to take, the more lost you will get.

Choosing the wrong identity can cripple you. When I labeled myself an introvert as a young man, I allowed myself to use introverted excuses to procrastinate on my big goals.

Choosing the wrong identity can cripple you.

If you tell yourself, "I'm not a morning person," you'll allow unhelpful behavior to support this, such as staying up late watching Netflix, drinking too much wine in the evening, hitting the snooze button, and avoiding morning focus work.

But that identity does not serve you—it destroys you.

Changing Your Story to Change Your Identity

My friend Bedros Keuilian often says, "Change your story, and you change your identity." Many of us are trapped by false narratives shaped by past trauma. These stories become self-fulfilling prophecies, driving the financial, fitness, faith, and family struggles we face today. But here's the truth: as the storyteller, you can rewrite the narrative whenever you choose.

- Change your story.
- Change your beliefs.
- Change your identity.
- Gather evidence to support the new you.

Personal Integrity: The Root of Discipline

"What you do is who you are."

Tim Grover, one of the greatest mindset coaches, taught me a lesson that changed my life: **Pressure is a privilege.**

In 2018, I hired Tim to speak at one of my coaching events. Tim is relentless. He attended the entire 3-day event, signed four hundred books the night before, and delivered a powerful session. During the Q&A with Tim, a young man stood up and began criticizing Tim's stories and style. Under pressure, Tim remained graceful and composed, demonstrating the very principles he teaches. Later, I apologized to Tim, but he told me, "Pressure is a privilege. The higher you go, the more people want to knock you down."

Discipline and standards allow you to handle pressure with grace. They align your actions with your identity, keeping you steady no matter what comes your way. When you commit to living by your standards, you won't just survive pressure—you'll thrive under it.

Identity: Who You are is What You Do

I'm a family man and a father before I'm an author. If my daughter needs me at 4:00 a.m., writing takes a backseat. Being the best father I can be takes precedence over trends like exercising twice a day, reading twenty pages, or cold plunging. My identity reflects my priorities.

17

The Ultimate Identity Exercise: Reprogram Your Mind for Success

Step 1: Gratitude and Evidence
Write down three things you're grateful for right now. List three personal wins that prove your discipline and capability.

Step 2: Identity Declaration
Write this sentence: "I am [insert who you want to become]." Follow it with actions: "I prove this by [insert small, consistent habits]."

The Ultimate Identity Exercise: Reprogram Your Mind for Success

Step 3: Future Vision
Write your top three goals for the next 12 months. Beneath each goal, explain why achieving it matters and how it aligns with your identity.

Step 4: The Promise
Make one promise to yourself today that reinforces your new identity. Write it down and commit to it.

We have created a downloadable worksheet for you to build your identity. Visit DarkSideOfDiscipline.com/success or use this QR code to access it for free.

Remind Yourself: Anchoring to Your Identity

> You may encounter many defeats, but you must not be defeated. In fact, it may be necessary to encounter the defeats so you can know who you are, what you can rise from, how you can still come out of it.
> —*Maya Angelou*

As you grow in self-discipline and eliminate long-term suffering from your life, there will inevitably be moments of challenge—times when it feels like you're suffering.

These moments are not setbacks; they are opportunities to strengthen your identity and align with your standards.

For me, these moments often arise during sleepless nights when my children need me. It feels like suffering when all I want is rest, but those times are reminders of who I am: a father committed to being present for his children. Similarly, when you're detoxing from a sugar addiction, building better nutrition habits, or pushing your body through a tough workout, the short-term pain can feel overwhelming. Yet, it's through these challenges that you reinforce your identity and maintain your standards.

The Power of an Anchor Phrase

During moments of stress or temptation, having an anchor phrase—a mantra, affirmation, or guiding statement—can make all the difference. This phrase brings you back to your Big Why, focusing your energy on what truly matters and helping you resist distractions or toxic temptations. It's a simple yet powerful tool for staying aligned with your identity.

For me, my anchor phrase is: **Everything for my family.**

When I want to sleep in and risk falling behind at work, I remind myself that it could jeopardize my family's future. When I'm tempted to skip a hard workout, I remind myself that my training is for my kids—to be a fit father who can outlast their boundless energy. This phrase anchors me to the identity I've committed to.

Strengthening Your Identity with a Theme for Life

You've already made a commitment to being a certain type of person. A theme for your year, or even for your life, becomes the icing on the identity cake. For me, my identity statement is simple yet profound:

I am a polite and courteous person. I do not drink or swear. I am a good father and a loving husband, and I do everything to provide a good life for my wife and kids.

This belief system shapes every decision I make. It's why I can wake up at 1:00 a.m. to feed a hungry baby without a second thought. That's why skipping exercise or eating poorly is not an option. My decisions are rooted in the long-term vision I have for my family and my life.

The Straight Line to Success

Unlike fleeting trends or external motivators, my identity and standards keep me grounded. I don't need cold plunges, a Navy SEAL yelling in my face, or a t-shirt to validate my discipline. My choices are not about earning gold stars from strangers on the internet.

Instead, I focus on being the man my wife and kids need me to be. My identity and standards are my compass, guiding every decision and ensuring I stay on the straight line to success.

When you align your actions with your identity and reinforce it with a powerful theme, you create a life of integrity and purpose—not for external validation, but because it's simply who you are.

18

Standards: The Hidden Force that Shapes Your Destiny

> If you have a standard for everything you do,
> it makes decision-making a lot easier.
> —*Oprah Winfrey*

In 2019, at the Annual Fit Body Boot Camp World Conference, I, Daniel Woodrum, sat in the audience captivated as entrepreneur and motivational speaker Ed Mylett shared a story that changed my life. He described his vision of meeting God after he died. In this vision, God introduces him to the person he was meant to become. "Ed, here is the man I designed you to be," God would say. "This was the man, husband, father, and businessman you had the full potential to become. But here's who you actually became."

Ed's eyes filled with tears on stage as he admitted that nothing drives him more than fulfilling his potential—closing the gap between who he is and who he could be. Hearing him speak with such conviction about his purpose struck a deep chord in me. That day, something shifted.

For those striving for success, several elements can help us reach our potential: Goals, Vision, Mindset, Work Ethic, and Environment. But if there's one factor that transforms everything else, it's Standards. As Ed said that day, "You get the standard you accept. You get to decide."

Standards: Your Framework for Life

Standards are not preferences or suggestions; they're the non-negotiables that define our lives. They shape our future and influence every decision we make. Show me your standards, and I'll show you your destiny. True success and fulfillment don't come from intense bursts of discipline when it's convenient; they come from the quiet, steady commitment to your standards—day after day, no matter the circumstances.

My mentor and co-author, Craig Ballantyne, embodies this principle. Craig has built his life on foundational standards. He doesn't swear. He doesn't snooze. He doesn't drink alcohol. He doesn't engage in drama. These rules aren't limitations but anchors, keeping him aligned with the person he wants to be. No matter what the day brings, Craig holds to these standards, letting them guide him.

As Pittsburgh Steelers head coach Mike Tomlin famously declares, "The Standard is the Standard." No one in NFL history has embodied that standard of excellence more consistently. With an unprecedented 18 consecutive (and counting) non-losing seasons—the longest streak ever to start an NFL coaching career—Tomlin has redefined what it means to lead with unwavering discipline and unshakable standards.

His success isn't built on chasing fleeting talent but on instilling a culture of accountability, resilience, and relentless execution. Inside the Steelers' facility, core values like Respect, Integrity, Humility, Family, and Grit aren't just words on a wall—they are the foundation of a dynasty of consistency. In a league where coaching tenures are often short-lived and turbulent, Tomlin's record stands as a testament to the power of elite leadership, proving that true greatness isn't about flashes of brilliance but about standards and a strong identity.

Whether you're a coach, CEO, professional, or parent, establishing your own standards is one of the most powerful steps you can take toward reaching your full potential.

The Power of Standards

By setting personal standards, you build confidence because consistency builds trust with yourself. Standards also help you hit your goals because consistent actions over time yield results. They simplify decision-making—when you live by rules you create, there's less mental fatigue. You gain self-control, conserve willpower, and attract people who are also steady and reliable.

Life will always throw challenges your way, but the one thing you can control is your standards. They become your unshakable foundation.

However, your standards must be your own. They need to align with your purpose and values. Emulating others' standards is like wearing a suit that doesn't fit; it won't work. I learned this lesson the hard way when I tried to adopt Craig's "no swearing" standard. While I respected him, the standard didn't resonate with me personally. Standards only work if they are meaningful to you.

Standards as Laws, Not Systems

Standards are like breathing. You don't need motivation to breathe. Breathing is a rule of life, a law, like gravity. Systems can break, but standards—when ingrained as laws—become unbreakable. They govern your actions without exception.

> ### Craig's 12 Rules for His Life
>
> Whatever rules you have adopted, abide by them as laws, and as if you would be a sinner to transgress them; and do not regard what anyone says of you, for this, after all, is no concern of yours.
>
> —*Epictetus*
>
> I first wrote my "Rules for Living" on Easter Sunday, 2011. I realized I had an operating system and wanted to document it for my coaching clients who often asked, "What Would Craig Do?"
>
> These rules are my Standards and Identity and make the right actions automatic, so I don't have to waste time on making decisions about discipline.
>
> 1. I go to bed and get up at the same time seven days per week (8 p.m. and 4 a.m., respectively). I stick to my diet, avoid caffeine after 1 p.m., and avoid alcohol within three hours of bedtime. (Note: I quit drinking alcohol in 2021.)
> 2. I write for at least sixty minutes first thing every morning.
> 3. I do not check email before 9:00 a.m., and I do not talk on the phone unless it is a scheduled interview or conference call.
> 4. I act polite and courteous, and I do not swear.

5. I create a to-do list at the start and end of every workday and update my daily gratitude and achievement journal.
6. I do not engage in confrontations with anyone, in person or online. This is a waste of time and energy. If I have caused harm, I apologize and fix the situation. And then, I take a deep breath, relax, breathe out, and re-focus my efforts back on my work and goals.
7. I am guided by these two phrases:
   a. "Nothing matters." I can only work towards my big goals and my vision of helping others while the opinions of others do not matter.
   b. "It will all be over soon." Everything, both good and bad, comes to an end. I must enjoy the good while it lasts and persevere through the bad until I have beaten it.
8. Everything that happens to me—good and bad—is my personal responsibility. I blame no one but myself. These are the choices I've made; this is the life I'm living. I accept the consequences of my actions.
9. I will help ten million men and women transform their lives.
10. I will not be the person I don't want to be. I will not be petty, jealous, envious, or give in to any other of those lazy emotions. I will not gossip or speak badly of others, no matter who I am with or what environment I am in. I will not be negative when it is easier to be positive. I will not hurt others when it is possible to help. I will know the temptations, situations, and environments in life that I must avoid, and I will, in fact, avoid them, even if it means loosening relationships with others who "live" in those environments. It's my life, and that matters more than what other people think of me.

11. "I will always keep the child within me alive." (Credit to Frank McKinney.) I will make time to laugh and play every day.
12. "I will write with honesty and feeling." (Credit to Ted Nicholas.) The opinion of others does not matter. What matters is the number of people that I can help by sharing advice and encouragement in my writing.

My 12 Rules have made me much happier and have eliminated much of the stress in my life.

There will be two types of reactions to the idea of rules. First, some will dismiss it and dismiss me. The point of the list is not for you to sit there and think, "What a loser. He is so boring." The reason for sharing my standards is to stimulate the creation of your standards so that you make better decisions in your life.

19

Building Your Unbreakable Standards System: The Final Evolution beyond Discipline

After hearing Ed Mylett's talk, Daniel Woodrum developed a simple system to help people create their own standards. Follow his four steps to design standards that bring clarity, success, and fulfillment:

1. Identify Your Quadrants

Determine the four areas of life that matter most. These can be personal, professional, or a mix of both.

My Examples:

- Family
- Health
- Discipline
- Leadership

2. Define Your Mission Statements

For each quadrant, write two to three sentences that explain why it's essential. This provides clarity and purpose for your standards. Here are my mission statements:

Family Mission Statement:
My family comes before anything else in life. They are my #1 priority and take precedence over any and everything else in this world.

Health Mission Statement:
My health is the greatest asset I have that will not only influence my wealth but has a direct impact on my family. I want to be the Gold Standard Example for my kids of what a healthy dad looks and acts like.

Discipline Mission Statement:
Discipline is my greatest superpower. When I create systems that protect my time, focus, and energy, I am truly unstoppable, and nobody can compete with me.

Leadership Mission Statement:
Everything that transpires in my life is happening "for" me. I must always take full responsibility and lead by example for others. This means embracing challenges and never shying away from tough times and conversations.

3. Create Three Standards per Quadrant

Based on your mission statements, establish three specific standards for each area. These standards become the core habits and values that guide your actions. Here are my 12 total personal standards:

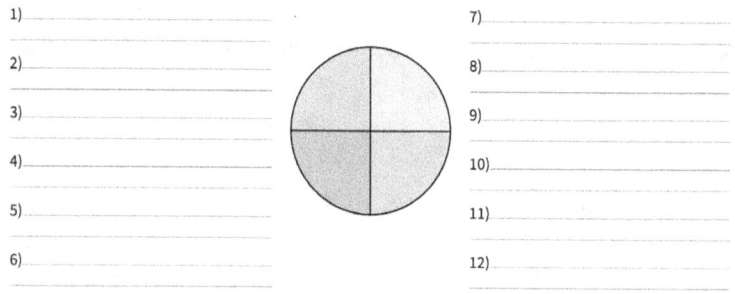

The 12 Standards of My Life chart.

Family Standards:

1. Tell my family I love them daily.
2. Don't make non-family commitments after 4:00 p.m.
3. Always operate as #TeamWoodrum.

Health Standards:

1. 20 minutes of strenuous exercise daily
2. Walk 30 minutes daily
3. Limit coffee to two cups daily.

Discipline Standards:

1. Follow my bedtime routine.
2. Don't hit the snooze button.
3. Limit social media to thirty minutes per day.

Leadership Standards:

1. Take extreme ownership of everything.
2. Embrace tough conversations.
3. Always praise others.

4. Create Accountability

Share your standards with a few trusted individuals—your "Trust Tribe"—and ask for accountability. Display your standards somewhere visible as a daily reminder.

My Trust Tribe:

- My wife, Brittney
- My mentor, Craig Ballantyne
- Early To Rise Coaches Gavin McHale & Galel Fajardo

Accountability Practices:

- I regularly discuss my progress with my Trust Tribe.
- I display my standards on my phone screen saver.

Establishing standards takes time, and it's about progress, not perfection. With consistency, they'll become effortless and provide a clear path to sustained success.

> ## Marcus vs. Chuck: The Power of Standards and Identity
>
> The difference between Marcus and Chuck wasn't their discipline. The difference was clarity. Marcus knew what he wanted and set his standards accordingly, while Chuck never did. Marcus focused on the end goal; Chuck got lost chasing the means to an undefined end.
>
> Marcus operates automatically, guided by standards that protect him. His decisions aren't burdensome because his identity and standards dictate his actions. Chuck, on the other hand, white-knuckles through life, chasing the Discipline Dragon on dangerous detours in the wrong direction. His lack of clarity and standards drained his energy and destroyed his family.
>
> Today, many of us stand where Chuck did at the start of his journey, caught in the trap of chasing other people's definitions of success. But we have the opportunity to choose our own path.
>
> **Chasing other people's definitions of success is the least disciplined thing you can do.**
>
> Blindly adding tasks or following trends without reflection leads to the dark side of discipline: burnout, frustration, and failure. Instead, define what success means to you. Choose your path, commit to it, and never give up on what truly matters.
>
> From this path, you'll shift your identity, set higher standards for yourself, and make a big leap towards achieving your big goals and dreams that matter to you.

20

Beyond Discipline: Stop Chasing. Suffer Less. Achieve More.

As Chuck found out, the Dark Side of Discipline can destroy your dreams.

It's no secret that when you join a discipline challenge, it fires you up.

But it's a dark secret, and one that most won't admit, that when they complete the challenge or when the challenge ends prematurely due to failure, all the momentum, motivation, and even transformation halts. And if all of this effort is in the wrong direction in the first place, you're worse off than you started.

You chase. You suffer. You achieve less.

It's time to call this out for what it is—distraction, not discipline.

On the other hand, Marcus learned that evolving beyond the animal instinct to do "hard things" and living life according to personal standards can set you free.

You've come to a fork in the road.

Keep doing what you're doing, and get the results (or lack thereof) that you always have.

Or shift to creating the systems and standards you need to achieve your big goals and dreams.

The moment you put this book down, you have a choice. Will this be just another book you read and forget? Or will this be the book that changes everything?

As you go, so goes your family, your team at work, and even your friends.

If you want them chasing, suffering, and not reaching their full potential, then, by all means, keep flipping and flopping from challenge to challenge. That's what they'll do too.

But if you want them to get on the straight line to success, take action on the steps we've given you in this book.

- Build your Big Why.
- Set a specific definition of success that is right for you.
- Eliminate your Doom Loops.
- Create effortless discipline systems.
- Strengthen your identity daily.
- And set eternal standards for high performance.

When it comes to family, "Behaviors are caught, not taught." What your children and team members (at work) see you do is what they will see as acceptable for them too.

It is your responsibility as a parent and leader to lead by example, pursue only the goals that matter to you and them, and commit to continuous and never-ending improvement. This is your moment.

Your Specific Definition of Success

Close your eyes and picture the person you want to become. Picture the life you've been working toward. Not just in fleeting moments but in every detail—the way you move, the way you speak, the way you lead. Picture the pride in your family's eyes, the admiration of your peers, and the quiet confidence that radiates from within.

> *Picture yourself a year from now, standing tall, knowing that every decision you've made has brought you closer to your best self. You're no longer drained, no longer doubting—you're dominating. And the people around you? They're inspired by the unstoppable force you've become.*

This is the life that's waiting for you. You can feel it, can't you? Now, reach for it. The only thing standing between you and that vision is the choice to commit—fully, relentlessly—to your standards.

You are not the person you were when you started this book.

You've stepped into a new identity—someone who no longer chases discipline but commands their life through unshakable standards. Now, declare it boldly.

> *I will rise above. I will no longer chase discipline—I will live by my personal standards. I am the person who shows up, thrives under pressure, and makes no excuses. The life I want is mine to create, and I will not settle for less. Every day, I am*

becoming the person I was meant to be. I lead myself. I lead my family. I lead my legacy. And I refuse to back down from the responsibility of greatness.

Write this out. Post it at your desk. Put it on the front page of your journal. More importantly, live by it. Standards are not goals—they are laws. They are non-negotiable.

Let this playbook be your foundation, your guide, and your unwavering compass.

Amateurs chase other people's definitions of discipline.

Professionals set higher personal standards in alignment with their big why, values, and vision, and this drives every decision.

Time for you to turn pro.

Stop chasing. Suffer less. Achieve more.

Bibliography

James Clear. *Atomic Habits: An Easy & Proven Way to Build Good Habits & Break Bad Ones.* New York: Avery, 2018.

Tim Grover. *Winning: The Unforgiving Race to Greatness.* New York: Scribner, 2021.

Tony Robbins. *Awaken the Giant Within: How to Take Immediate Control of Your Mental, Emotional, Physical and Financial Destiny!* New York: Simon & Schuster, 1992.

Tim Grover. *Relentless: From Good to Great to Unstoppable.* New York: Scribner, 2013.

Aron Ralston. *Between a Rock and a Hard Place.* New York: Atria, 2004.

Epictetus. *The Art of Living: The Classical Manual on Virtue, Happiness and Effectiveness.* Edited by Sharon Lebell. New York: HarperOne, 2007.

Craig Ballantyne. *Unstoppable: How to Get Through Hell, Overcome Anxiety, and Dominate in Business and Life.* Carson City, NV: Lioncrest Publishing, 2018.

Peter Attia. *Outlive: The Science and Art of Longevity.* New York: Harmony, 2023.

Rock N' Roll True Stories 2. *Guns N' Roses Axl Rose On How He Gets Ready for a Show.* YouTube.com. https://youtu.be/DhqmJcQ8eUA?feature=shared.

Lewis Howes. *The School of Greatness: A Real-World Guide to Living Bigger, Loving Deeper, and Leaving a Legacy.* Emmaus, PA: Rodale, 2015.

Craig Ballantyne. *The Perfect Day Formula. How to Own the Day and Control Your Life.* Carson City, NV: Lioncrest Publishing, 2016.

Mel Robbins. *The 5 Second Rule: Transform Your Life, Work, and Confidence with Everyday Courage.* New York: Savio Republic, 2024.

Jon Gordon. *You Win in the Locker Room First: The 7 Cs to Build a Winning Team in Business, Sports, and Life.* Hoboken, NJ: Wiley, 2015.

John C. Maxwell. *The 21 Irrefutable Laws of Leadership: Follow Them and People Will Follow You.* New York: HarperCollins Leadership, 1998 and 2007.

Bibliography

Peter Thiel. *Zero to One: Notes on Startups, or How to Build the Future.* New York: Currency, 2014.

McKinney, Frank. *Aspirational Thoughts—Inspirational Images.* Boynton Beach, FL: Caring House, 2024;

McKinney, Frank. *Aspire! How to Create Your Own Reality and Alter Your DNA.* Boynton Beach, FL: Caring House, 2021.

About the Authors

Craig Ballantyne is known as the "World's Most Disciplined Man" and is a business coach for high-performing entrepreneurs who want to go to the next level. His previous books include *The Perfect Day Formula*, *The Perfect Week Formula*, and his *Wall Street Journal* bestseller, *Unstoppable*. He was also the creator of the Turbulence Training fitness system and owns EarlyToRise.com. Craig lives in Vancouver, Canada, with his wife, Michelle, and three children.

Daniel Woodrum is an entrepreneur, coach, and discipline expert dedicated to helping business owners and high performers reach their full potential. As the Head Coach at Early To Rise, Daniel has spent over a decade leading teams and coaching thousands of entrepreneurs to achieve greater discipline, leadership, and productivity. With over 14 years of entrepreneurial experience, Daniel has owned multiple businesses and guided countless high-achievers to elevate their standards, systems, and results. Daniel lives in Charleston, South Carolina, with his wife Brittney and their three children, Blease, Banks, and Bellamy.

CONNECT WITH CRAIG & DANIEL

Follow them on Instagram today.

@REALCRAIGBALLANTYNE

@DANIEL_LEE_WOODRUM

Enjoy Craig's Other Books

AVAILABLE WHEREVER BOOKS ARE SOLD

THIS BOOK IS PROTECTED INTELLECTUAL PROPERTY

The author of this book values Intellectual Property and has utilized Instant IP, a groundbreaking technology. Instant IP is the patented, blockchain-based solution for Intellectual Property protection.

Blockchain is a distributed public digital record that can not be edited. Instant IP timestamps the author's ideas, creating a smart contract, thus an immutable digital asset that proves ownership and establishes a first to use / first to file event.

Protected by Instant IP ™

LEARN MORE AT INSTANTIP.TODAY

www.ingramcontent.com/pod-product-compliance
Lightning Source LLC
Chambersburg PA
CBHW052143070526
44585CB00017B/1958